Headway

D1394222

Academic Skills
Reading, Writing, and Study Skills

INTRODUCTORY LEVEL **Student's Book**

Sarah Philpot and Lesley Curnick
Series Editors: Liz and John Soars

OXFORD

CONTENTS

1 Meeting people

READING New people

1 Work with a partner. Look at the webpage and the photos. Answer the questions. `Read STUDY SKILL`

   1 What is the club?
   2 How many photos of people are there?
   3 How many men are there in the photos?
   4 How many paragraphs are there?

> **STUDY SKILL** Surveying
>
> Before you read a text, look at the page quickly. Ask:
> - What is the title?
> - What do the pictures show?
> - How many paragraphs are there?
>
> The answers help you understand what a text is about.

University Internet Chess Club

| ABOUT THE CLUB | EVENTS | NEW MEMBERS |

New Members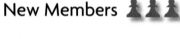

 My name is **Miguel Sousa**. I come from Rio de Janeiro, in Brazil, and I am a lecturer. I play chess with my son.

 My name is **Mona Patel**. I come from Delhi, in India. I'm a medical student. I like chess very much.

 I am **Jane Day**. I come from Sydney, in Australia. I am an English Language teacher. I am a beginner.

 I am **Deniz Osman**. I live in Ankara, in Turkey. I am a student. I play chess with my friends.

a

b

c

d

2 Read the webpage. Write the names under the photos. Check your answers with a partner.

3 Read the webpage again. Answer the questions.

   1 Which country does **Miguel** come from?
   2 What does he do?
   3 Which city does **Jane** come from?
   4 What does she do?
   5 Which city does **Deniz** come from?
   6 What does he do?
   7 Which country does **Mona** come from?
   8 What does she do?

4 Survey the webpage below. Answer the questions.
  1 What is the club?
  2 How many people are there in the photos?
  3 How many paragraphs are there?

www.onlinebookclub.com

ONLINE Book Club

| ABOUT US | BOOKS | NEW MEMBERS | EVENTS |

New Members

1 **Peter Blake** <u>comes</u> from New York. He (is) an engineer. He is married and has one daughter. He likes reading very much.

2 **Ada** and **Ninoy Manlapaz** come from Manila, in the Philippines. They are teachers. They are married and they have two children. They read a lot of books.

a

b

5 Read about the new members. Answer the questions.
  1 Which paragraph is about people from the Philippines?
  2 Which paragraph is about a person from the USA?

6 Write the names of the people under the photos. Check your answers with a partner.

7 Read the rules. Work with a partner. Read the webpage again.
  1 (Circle) forms of the verb *be*.
  2 <u>Underline</u> the other verbs.

RULES Present Simple (1)

Use the Present Simple to give facts (true information).

The verb *be*

I	am	
He / She / It	**is**	*a teacher.*
We / You / They	**are**	*students.*

Other verbs

I / You / We / They	come	
He / She / It	come**s**	*from Delhi.*

KEY LANGUAGE The alphabet

1 Write the correct small letter next to the capital letter. Check your answers with a partner.

c s y e k v u p x i d n o g b q w t a r m f h z j l

A _a_   **B** _   **C** _   **D** _   **E** _   **F** _   **G** _   **H** _   **I** _

J _   **K** _   **L** _   **M** _   **N** _   **O** _   **P** _   **Q** _   **R** _

S _   **T** _   **U** _   **V** _   **W** _   **X** _   **Y** _   **Z** _

2 **Read STUDY SKILL** (Circle) the five vowels in exercise 1. Check your answers with a partner.

> **STUDY SKILL** The alphabet
>
> The alphabet has 26 letters. There are 21 consonants, for example, *b, c, n, t*. There are five vowels, for example, *a, o*.
>
> Knowing the alphabet helps you:
> - find words in a dictionary
> - record vocabulary in a notebook or computer file

3 Work with a partner. Write the words in alphabetical order.

1 _____
2 _____
3 _____
4 _____
5 _____
6 _____

| lecturer |
| student |
| teacher |
| doctor |
| dentist |
| engineer |

4 Look at the registration desk for a conference. Where do these people go to register?

1 Heinz **Ehrhardt**   E–H
2 Franco **Corelli**
3 Stella **Roberts**
4 Gabriella **Vancak**
5 Abdul **Osman**
6 Hussein **Ibrahim**

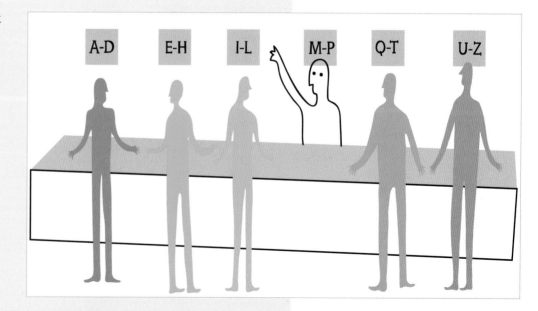

A-D   E-H   I-L   M-P   Q-T   U-Z

WRITING Introductions

1 Read the rules. Complete the sentences about you.

> My name is …
> I come from …
> I am a(n) …

2 Work with a partner. Ask and answer the questions. Make notes.

1 What is your name?
2 Where do you come from?
3 What do you do?

3 Write a paragraph about your partner.

> My partner's name is … She/He …

4 `Read STUDY SKILL` Read the paragraph. (Circle) the capital letters.

Adul Suttikul and **Boonwat Mookjai** come from Bangkok, in Thailand. They are computer engineering students. Adul is 20 and Boonwat is 21.

5 Read the student's paragraph about Max. Add six capital letters and three full stops.

> max comes from frankfurt in germany he is a doctor he is married and has three children

Check your answers with a partner.

6 `Read STUDY SKILL` Read about the Hussein family. Correct the mistakes.

> My husband and I come from Dubai. I am a housewife, and my husband <u>am</u> a computer programmer. He <u>work</u> in <u>a</u> office. We <u>has</u> two children. Ahmed is four and Layla <u>are</u> six. Layla <u>go</u> to <u>a</u> international school.

RULES Articles *a* and *an*

Use *a* before a word beginning with a consonant:
a doctor   **a s**tudent

Use *an* before a word beginning with a vowel sound:
an engineer   **an a**ccountant

STUDY SKILL Punctuation (1)

Use CAPITAL LETTERS for:
- the start of sentences: *He is a doctor.*
- names of people and places: *Jane, Brazil.*
- the pronoun *I*: *Jane and **I** come from Australia.*

End sentences with a full stop (.).

STUDY SKILL Checking your writing (1)

It is important to check your writing for mistakes. Check:
- the subject and the verb:
  He go to university. ✗   *He goes to university.* ✓
- articles:
  She is a engineer. ✗   *She is an engineer.* ✓

VOCABULARY DEVELOPMENT Instructions

1 | Read STUDY SKILL | Label the pictures and examples 1–10 with instruction words from the box.

> **STUDY SKILL** Following instructions
>
> It is necessary to read and follow instructions carefully. Make sure you know the important words, e.g. *underline*.

2 Work with a partner. Follow the instructions.

1 <u>Underline</u> the verb.

> She works at a school.

2 (Circle) the country.

> He comes from New Zealand.

3 Label the picture with the correct words.

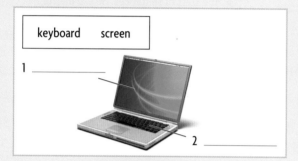

keyboard   screen

1 _____

2 _____

4 Match the capital letters with the small letters.

1 [G]   h
2 [H]   i
3 [I]   g

5 Number the countries in alphabetical order.

- [ ] Japan
- [ ] Thailand
- [ ] India

Letters, words, and sentences

3 Write the words from the box next to examples 1–7.

> consonants   ~~letters~~   nouns   a sentence
> verbs   vowels   a word

1 <u>letters</u>_____ a, b, c, d
2 _____ a, e, i
3 _____ l, m, n
4 _____ international
5 _____ students, doctors
6 _____ write, read, understand
7 _____ I come from London.

4 Look at exercise 3 again. Add one more example for 1–7.

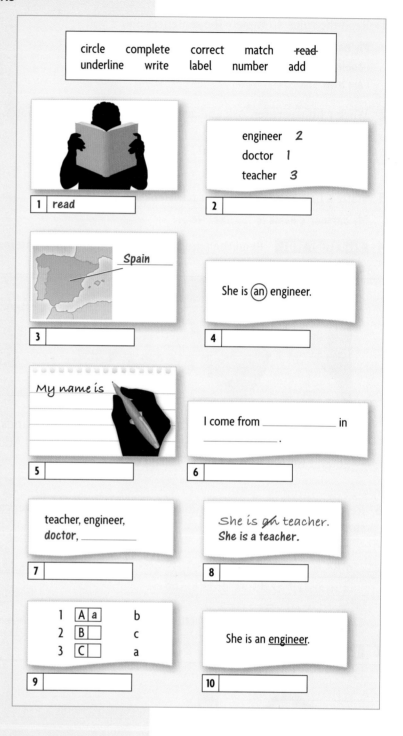

circle   complete   correct   match   ~~read~~
underline   write   label   number   add

1 read

2

engineer   2
doctor   1
teacher   3

Spain

3

4

She is (an) engineer.

My name is

5

6

I come from _____ in
_____ .

teacher, engineer,
doctor, _____

7

8

She is ~~an~~ teacher.
She is a teacher.

1 [A | a]   b
2 [B |]   c
3 [C |]   a

9

10

She is an <u>engineer</u>.

REVIEW

1 Survey the webpage and answer the questions.

   1 What is the club?
   2 How many paragraphs are there?
   3 How many new members are there?

University Backgammon Club

| ABOUT THE CLUB | RULES | NEW MEMBERS | EVENTS |

New Members

My name is **Karim Mansour**. I come from Rabat, in Morocco. I study engineering at university. I play backgammon with my friends.

I am **Anna Costa**. I live in Rio de Janeiro, in Brazil. I am a nurse. I work in a hospital. I am married, and I play backgammon with my husband.

2 Read the webpage and answer the questions.

   1 What country does **Karim** come from?
   2 What city does he come from?
   3 What does he study?
   4 Where does he study?
   5 Where does **Anna** live?
   6 What does she do?
   7 Where does she work?

3 Read the webpage again. Circle forms of the verb *be* and underline the other verbs. Check your answers with a partner.

4 Read the student's paragraph below and find:

- three mistakes with verbs
- two mistakes with punctuation
- two mistakes with articles

> My family and I comes from London My father is a architect and my mother am a businesswoman. I has one brother. he is 18 and he is an student.

5 Write a paragraph about a member of your family. Write about where they live and their occupation.

My uncle's/father's/sister's name is ... He/She ...

6 Check your writing for:

- Present Simple verbs
- capital letters and full stops
- articles (*a /an*)

2 Countries

READING Mountains, seas, and rivers

1 Label the map (1–4) with words from the box. Check your answers with a partner.

coastline	mountains	river	East

2 **Read STUDY SKILL** Survey the pictures and the title of the text. What is the text about?

a) the weather in Spain
b) the land in Spain
c) the people in Spain

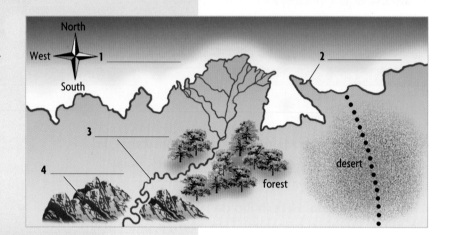

STUDY SKILL Predicting

Before you read a text, look at the pictures and title, and predict what it is about. This:

- prepares you for reading
- helps you understand the text

Spain
The geography of Spain

Spain is a large country in the south of Europe. It has borders with France, Andorra, and Portugal. It has a long coastline on the Mediterranean Sea, and a short coastline on the Atlantic Ocean. There are mountains in Spain, but there is a lot of flat land, too. There are two important rivers, the Tajo and the Ebro. The capital city is Madrid, in the centre of the country. Barcelona is the second city of Spain, and it is on the Mediterranean coast.

Location

Flag

Flat land in Spain

3 Read the text quickly. Check your answer to exercise 2.

4 Read the text about Spain again. Answer the questions.

1 Where is Spain?
2 How many countries does Spain border?
3 Are there mountains in Spain?
4 What are the names of the rivers?
5 What is the capital city of Spain?

Check your answers with a partner.

5 Work with a partner. Survey the pictures and the title of the text below. What is the text about?

6 Read the text to check your ideas.

Algeria: a large country

Algerian desert

Algiers

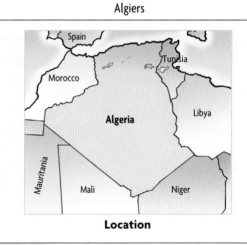

Location

Algeria is a very large country in North Africa. It has borders with Morocco, Mauritania, Western Sahara, Mali, Niger, Libya, and Tunisia. In the north, it has a long coastline on the Mediterranean Sea. Most of Algeria is mountains and desert, but ¹_____ an area of flat land along the coast. ²_____ two important rivers in Algeria, the Chelif and the Seybouse. The capital of Algeria is Algiers, and it is in the north, on the Mediterranean Sea.

7 Read the rules. Complete the text about Algeria with *there is* or *there are*. Check your answers with a partner.

8 Read the text about Algeria again. Are the sentences true (**T**) or false (**F**)?

1 Algeria is in East Africa.   F
2 It has borders with eight other countries.
3 It is on the Mediterranean Sea.
4 Algeria has two important rivers.
5 The capital city is in the south of the country.

9 Work with a partner. Correct the false sentences.

1 Algeria is in North Africa.

RULES *there is / there are*

Use *there is* with one thing. For example:
There is *a lot of flat land.*

Use *there are* with two or more things. For example:
There are *mountains in Spain.*

WRITING My country

1 Look at the pairs of sentences. Is a) or b) better?

1 a) Turkey is in Europe. It is also in Asia.
   b) Turkey is in Europe, and it is also in Asia.

2 a) Switzerland has borders with five countries, but it does not have a coastline.
   b) Switzerland has borders with five countries. It does not have a coastline.

Compare your answers with a partner. **Read STUDY SKILL**

> ## STUDY SKILL Linking ideas (1)
>
> Linking ideas makes your writing clearer.
>
> - Use *and* to link similar ideas. For example:
>   a) *Barcelona is the second city of Spain.*
>   b) *It is on the Mediterranean coast.*
>   *Barcelona is the second city of Spain, **and** it is on the Mediterranean coast.*
>
> - Use *but* to link different ideas. For example:
>   a) *There are mountains in Spain.*
>   b) *There is a lot of flat land, too.*
>   *There are mountains in Spain, **but** there is a lot of flat land, too.*

2 Complete the sentences with *and* or *but*.

1 South Africa is a large country, _but_ Mali, Chad, and Angola are larger.
2 There are mountains in the east, ___ in the north it is flat.
3 Brasilia is the capital of Brazil, ___ São Paolo is bigger.
4 Adelaide is a state capital, ___ Canberra is the national capital.
5 Riyadh is the capital of Saudi Arabia, ___ it has a population of about five million people.

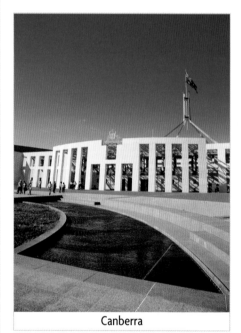

Canberra

Riyadh

3 **Read STUDY SKILL** Put commas in the student's sentences.

1 My country is hot dry and sunny.
2 Canberra Sydney and Melbourne are cities in Australia.
3 Spain exports cars medicines and oil.
4 Argentina has borders with Paraguay Brazil Bolivia Uruguay and Chile.

> ## STUDY SKILL Punctuation (2)
>
> Use commas (,) after words in a list. For example:
> - *It has borders with France, Andorra, and Portugal.*
> - *The capital city has many universities, technical institutes, colleges, and schools.*
>
> Using commas makes your writing easier to understand.

4 Read the text. Complete it with *and*, *but*, and two commas. Compare your answers with a partner.

My country

My country is Malaysia. It is in South-East Asia. It has borders with Thailand Brunei and Indonesia. It has coastlines on the South China Sea [1]_____ the Strait of Malacca. There is flat land around the coastline, [2]_____ there are mountains in the centre of the country. Over half the country has rainforests. The capital of Malaysia is Kuala Lumpur, [3]_____ it is a very modern city.

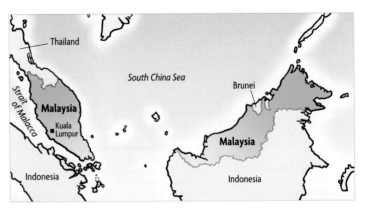

Malaysian rainforest

5 Answer the questions about your country.

1 What is the name of your country?
2 Where is your country?
3 What countries does it border?
4 Where are the coastlines?
5 Are there any mountains and rivers?
6 Is there a desert?
7 What is the capital city?

6 Write a paragraph about your country. Use your answers from exercise 5.

My country is … (name), and it is in … (part of the world)

7 Work with a partner. Check your partner's paragraph for:

- punctuation (capital letters, full stops, and commas)
- grammar (subject and verb agreement, articles)
- linking (*and*, *but*)

VOCABULARY DEVELOPMENT Alphabetical order

1 Work with a partner. Write the words in alphabetical order.

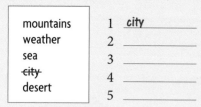

mountains	1	_city_
weather	2	_____
sea	3	_____
~~city~~	4	_____
desert	5	_____

2 Write the groups of words in alphabetical order.

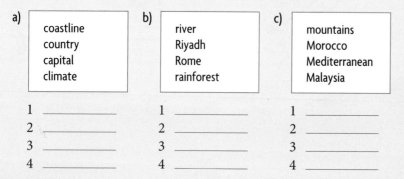

a)
| coastline |
| country |
| capital |
| climate |

1 _____
2 _____
3 _____
4 _____

b)
| river |
| Riyadh |
| Rome |
| rainforest |

1 _____
2 _____
3 _____
4 _____

c)
| mountains |
| Morocco |
| Mediterranean |
| Malaysia |

1 _____
2 _____
3 _____
4 _____

Parts of speech

3 **Read STUDY SKILL** Look at the dictionary entry and label:

- the meaning
- the part of speech
- the example

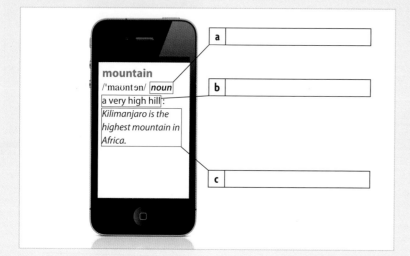

> **STUDY SKILL** Using a dictionary (1)
>
> A dictionary gives you information about words.
> For example:
> - the part of speech (noun, verb, or adjective)
> - the meaning
> - an example
>
> Good dictionary skills help your reading and writing.

4 Look at the sentences. Underline the nouns and circle the adjectives.

1 Spain is a large country.
2 It is dry in Mexico.
3 In my country, the land is flat.

5 Work with a partner. What part of speech are the underlined words?
Use a dictionary to check your answers.

1 There are a lot of <u>tourists</u> in Paris. *noun*
2 It is a <u>long</u> river.
3 The <u>city</u> is in the north.
4 Do you <u>like</u> travelling?
5 What countries does Italy <u>border</u>?

REVIEW

1 Work with a partner. Survey the pictures and the title. What is the text about?

a) the USA   b) Canada   c) Alaska

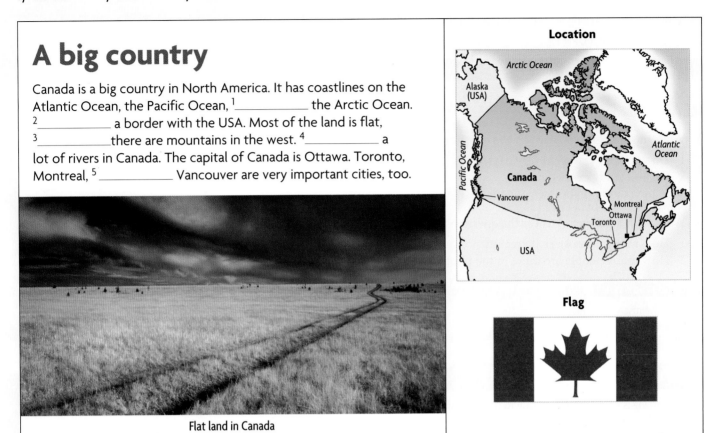

A big country

Canada is a big country in North America. It has coastlines on the Atlantic Ocean, the Pacific Ocean, [1]_____ the Arctic Ocean. [2]_____ a border with the USA. Most of the land is flat, [3]_____there are mountains in the west. [4]_____ a lot of rivers in Canada. The capital of Canada is Ottawa. Toronto, Montreal, [5]_____ Vancouver are very important cities, too.

Flat land in Canada

Location

Arctic Ocean

Alaska (USA)

Pacific Ocean

Atlantic Ocean

Canada

Vancouver

Montreal
Ottawa
Toronto

USA

Flag

2 Read the text quickly. Check your answer to exercise 1.

3 Read the text again. Complete it with words from the box.

and	and	but	There are	There is

4 Write the student's sentences with capital letters, commas, and full stops.

1 ottawa is the capital of canada
2 brazil is on the atlantic ocean
3 india has borders with pakistan china nepal burma bangladesh and bhutan
4 my country has mountains rivers and forests

5 Match questions 1–5 about New Zealand with answers a)–e).

1 ☐ Where is New Zealand?
2 ☐ What countries does it border?
3 ☐ What seas or oceans is it on?
4 ☐ Are there any mountains and rivers?
5 ☐ What is the capital city?

a) the South Pacific Ocean
b) in Oceania
c) Wellington
d) it has no borders
e) a lot of mountains / some flat land / a lot of rivers

6 Write a paragraph about New Zealand. Use the information in exercise 5.

New Zealand is in Oceania. It doesn't have any ...

3 Your studies

READING Every day

1 Work in small groups. Answer the questions.
1 Do you have lectures every day?
2 Do you study every day?
3 Which days do you see your friends?

2 Work with a partner. Answer the questions.
1 How many photos are there?
2 How many people are there in the photos?

3 `Read STUDY SKILL` Skim the text. Which paragraph is about …?
a) a chemistry student
b) a maths student
c) medical students

1

STUDY SKILL Skimming

Skimming is reading a text quickly to find general information, for example who the text is about.

2

University of **South London**

| COURSES | DEPARTMENT | STUDENT LIFE | CONTACT |

Meet our students

1 **Conrad Delzer** is 19. He is a chemistry student. He goes to the university every day. In the mornings, he works in the lab. At 12.30, he has lunch in the cafeteria. In the afternoons, he has lectures. He goes home at 5.00. In the evenings, he works on his computer and checks his emails.

2 **Malika Fahri** and **Yasmin Hamdi** study medicine. They have lectures in the mornings. They work in the lab in the afternoons. They go home at 6.00. In the evenings, they study at home. At the weekend, they see their friends.

3 **Martino Basti** gets up at 7.45. He leaves home and goes to the university at 8.15. Martino studies maths. He has lectures in the mornings, and he works on his computer in the afternoons. He does his homework and goes on the Internet in the evenings.

3

4 Write the names of the people under the photos.

5 Read the text on page 16. Work with a partner and answer the questions.

Conrad
1 How old is he?
2 Where does he have lunch?
3 What does he do in the afternoons?

Malika and Yasmin
4 When do they have lectures?
5 What do they do in the afternoons?
6 When do they see their friends?

Martino
7 When does he get up?
8 What does he do in the mornings?
9 When does he do his homework?

6 Work with a partner. Look at the two photos below. Answer the questions.
1 Where are the people?
2 What do they do?

a

b

7 Skim the text and look at the photos above. Which photo matches the text?

> **Dr Sudhir Mahoob** is a lecturer in business studies. He gives lectures at 9.00
> on Mondays and 11.30 on Thursdays. He works in his office in the afternoons.
> He does research. He uses his computer, and he reads books. He has seminars
> on Friday mornings. At the weekend, he plays with his children, and he goes
> to football matches.

8 Read the text. Are the sentences true (**T**) or false (**F**)?
Check your answers with a partner.

1 Dr Mahoob gives lectures on Mondays.
2 He works in the library in the afternoons.
3 On Friday mornings, he does research.
4 At the weekend, he goes to football matches.

KEY LANGUAGE Time

1 Write the times in the box under the clocks.
Compare your answers with a partner.

| 4.00 | 3.15 | 10.30 | 2.45 |

| a | | b | | c | | d | |

Time expressions

2 Read the rules. Circle five more time expressions with *at*, *in*, *on* in the text.
Compare your answers with a partner.

(On Saturdays,) Martino gets up at 8.00.
He goes to the gym in the mornings
and in the afternoons, he watches
TV. He likes sports programmes.
He visits his friends in the evenings.
He doesn't work at the weekend.

RULES Prepositions of time

We use different prepositions of time *in*, *at*, *on*
with different time expressions.

In a part of the day:
He watches television in the evenings.

At a time / the weekend:
At the weekend, he gets up at 8.30.

On a day, and a part of the day:
On Mondays, he teaches.
On Monday mornings, he gives a lecture.

---

3 Complete the sentences with *in*, *on*, and *at*.

1 Conrad gets up ____ 8.30 on Sundays.
2 He doesn't have lectures ____ Monday mornings.
3 ____ the weekend, Malika and Yasmin go on the Internet.
4 ____ the afternoons, the students have lectures.
5 Yasmin works in the library ____ Wednesdays.

Days of the week

4 Write the days of the week in the correct order. Use a capital letter at the
beginning of each day. Which days are the weekend in your country?

| Friday | ~~Monday~~ | Saturday | Sunday | Thursday | Tuesday | Wednesday |

Monday,

5 Find and underline four days of the week in exercises 2 and 3.

WRITING Your day

1 [Read STUDY SKILL] Complete the table with sentences 1–3.
Compare your answers with a partner.

1 Malika and Yasmin study medicine.
2 They use a computer.
3 Dr Mahoob reads books.

	subject	verb	object
1			
2			
3			

STUDY SKILL Writing sentences

A simple sentence has a subject, a verb, and an object.
A sentence starts with a capital letter and ends with
a full stop.

Martino studies maths.
subject   verb   object

2 Write the words in the correct order to make sentences.
Remember to start with a capital letter and end with a full stop.

1 studies / she / physics   *She studies physics.*
2 football / plays / he
3 do / their homework / they
4 his computer / he / uses
5 she / coffee / drinks

3 Complete the text with the verbs in the box.

I study nursing. I ¹_____ at 7.00 in the morning and
I ²_____ breakfast. I ³_____ the university at 8.00. I have
lectures in the mornings. I have lunch in the cafeteria at 12.00. In the
afternoons, I ⁴_____ in the lab. In the evenings, I work in the
library. I ⁵_____ the computers. I go home at 8.00 and have
dinner. I ⁶_____ television, and I ⁷_____ the Internet.

get up
go on
go to
have
use
watch
work

4 Answer the questions about you. Compare your answers with a partner.

1 What do you study?
2 When do you get up?
3 When is your first lecture?
4 Do you work in the library?
5 When do you have lunch?
6 What do you do in the evenings?
7 When do you go to bed?

5 Write a paragraph about your normal day.

I study .... I get up at ...

6 [Read STUDY SKILL] Work with a partner.
Correct the student's spelling mistake underlined in each sentence.

1 I go to work on <u>Wedenesdays</u>.
2 He watches television in the <u>evnings</u>.
3 Malika works in the <u>libry</u>.
4 She has lunch in the <u>cafetiria</u>.
5 Martino <u>gos</u> to the gym at the weekend.

STUDY SKILL Checking your writing (2)

Check your writing for spelling mistakes.
homwork ✗
homework ✓

If you use a computer, use the spell check tool:
■ Choose English as the language.
■ Look for words that are underlined in colour.

7 Work with a partner. Check your partner's paragraph from exercise 5
for spelling and punctuation mistakes.

VOCABULARY DEVELOPMENT Words that go together

1 [Read STUDY SKILL] Look at the pictures. Match the verbs with the nouns. Write the correct words under the pictures.

verbs	nouns
give	lunch
have	a lecture
read	a computer
use	a book

STUDY SKILL Recording vocabulary (1)

Some verbs and nouns go together, for example:

■ *watch + TV*

■ *study + medicine*

When you record vocabulary, make a note of words that go together.

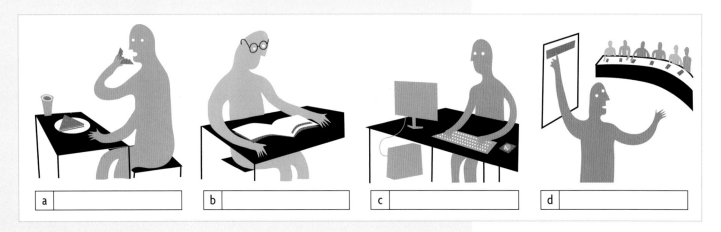

a _____ b _____ c _____ d _____

2 Circle the correct verb.
1 Tania *does / makes* her homework in the afternoons.
2 The students *have / do* some research in the library in the mornings.
3 Dr Miners *makes / gives* a seminar at 2.00.
4 Yann *reads / gives* articles on his computer.
5 Mario *does / has* dinner at 7.00.
6 Lara *visits / goes* friends at weekends.

3 Work in small groups. Add the verbs from the box to the nouns.

| check | give | go to | have | read | send | write |

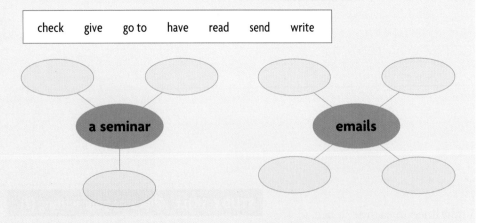

4 Complete the sentences with words from exercises 2 and 3 and a time expression. Compare your answers with a partner.
1 I check **my emails in the mornings.**
2 I send ...
3 I read ...
4 I do ...
5 I have ...
6 I write ...

REVIEW

1 Work with a partner. Look at the photos and answer the questions.
1 Where are the people?
2 Are they students or lecturers?

2 Skim the texts and match them to the photos. What do Paul and Tania study?

> **1** **Paul** studies engineering. Every day he gets up at 7.30 and goes to the university. He has lectures in the mornings. He has lunch at 1.00 and in the afternoons, he works in the computer centre. He goes home at 5.30. In the evenings, he works on his computer.

> **2** **Tania** is 20 years old. She studies Spanish and French. She works in the multimedia centre on Monday and Wednesday mornings. In the afternoons, she works in the library. She has lectures on Tuesday and Thursday afternoons. On Fridays, she visits her friends.

a

b

3 Work with a partner. Complete the questions with the correct preposition.
1 What does Paul do _____ 1.00?
2 What does he do _____ the afternoons?
3 What does Tania do _____ Wednesday mornings?
4 What does she do _____ Fridays?

4 Read the texts and answer the questions in exercise 3.

5 Look at the pictures. Match the verbs with the nouns. Write the correct words under the pictures.

verbs	nouns
drives	television
gives	to work
has	lunch
uses	a lecture
watches	his computer

What does Robert do on Wednesdays?

1   2   3   4   5

6 Write a paragraph about what Robert does on Wednesdays.
On Wednesdays, Robert works at the university. He drives to work at 8.00 and ...

7 Work with a partner. Check your partner's writing in exercise 6 for spelling and grammar mistakes.

READING SKILLS Finding important words • Scanning
WRITING SKILLS Linking ideas (2)
RESEARCH Using a search engine (1)
VOCABULARY DEVELOPMENT Recording vocabulary (2)

READING Where do they work?

1 Work in small groups. Answer the questions.

1	Do you work …?	a)	in the library	b)	at home	c) in the cafeteria
2	Do you work …?	a)	alone	b)	with a friend	c) with a group of friends
3	Do you work …?	a)	in silence	b)	with music	c) with the TV on

2 **Read STUDY SKILL** Read the sentences. Underline the important words.

1 <u>When</u> does he <u>arrive</u> at the <u>library</u>?
2 What is her job?
3 He studies engineering.
4 They work in a big office.
5 Where does she work?

Check your answers with a partner.

3 Read the title of the text on page 23. What is the text about?

a) work   b) study   c) free time

4 Read paragraph 1 of the text on page 23, and look at the photos below. Which photo matches the text?

STUDY SKILL Finding important words

In texts, underline the important words.
These are usually:

■ nouns, for example *job*
■ verbs, for example *studies*
■ adjectives, for example *big*

In questions, also underline the question word and think about what it means. For example:

■ *Where* tells you to look for a place.
■ *Why* tells you to look for a reason (*because*).

This helps you to find the information you need.

5 Read the questions and underline the important words. Compare your answers with a partner.

1 Where is the new research from?
2 Why are open-plan offices good?
3 What are the disadvantages of open-plan offices?
4 Why do people get ill more easily?
5 Do many companies think open-plan offices are good or bad?

6 **Read STUDY SKILL** Scan the text. Find and underline the important words from the questions in exercise 5. Check your answers with a partner.

7 Read the text and answer the questions in exercise 5.

STUDY SKILL Scanning

Scanning is reading quickly to find information.

Before you read, ask:
■ What information do you need?
■ What words in the text give you the information?

Scan the text to find these words and underline them.

Open-plan offices: new research

1 **The research**
People all around the world work in offices. Some people work in small offices for one or two people, but a lot of people now work in open-plan offices. In these offices, people work together in one big room. New research from Australia shows that there are advantages and disadvantages to these offices.

2 **What's good?**
The research shows three reasons to have open-plan offices. Firstly, in open-plan offices a lot of people can work in a small area. Secondly, it is easy for people to talk to work colleagues because they are in the same room. Finally, open-plan offices are cheaper for companies because they use less electricity.

3 **What's bad?**
The research also shows some disadvantages. Some people do not work well in open-plan offices because they are noisy. It is also difficult to talk privately in open-plan offices. Finally, researchers think that people get ill more easily because they work near each other.

4 **Open-plan offices – good or bad?**
The research concludes that there are advantages and disadvantages to open-plan offices, but many companies think that the advantages of having open-plan offices are greater than the disadvantages.

WRITING A good place to work

1 Look at the pairs of sentences. Is a) or b) better?

1 a) I like going to class. I meet my friends there.
   b) I like going to class because I meet my friends there.

2 a) It is difficult to work in open-plan offices because they are noisy.
   b) It is difficult to work in open-plan offices. They are noisy.

Compare your answers with a partner. **Read STUDY SKILL**

STUDY SKILL Linking ideas (2)

Use *because* to link ideas. It answers the question *Why?*
- **Why** *are open-plan offices cheaper?*
- *Open-plan offices are cheaper **because** they use less electricity.*

Linking ideas makes your writing clearer.

---

2 Match the start of a sentence with the correct ending. Link the sentences with *because*.

1	d	Learning English is important		a) it is quiet.
2	☐	The library is a good place to work		b) they want good jobs.
3	☐	Internet shopping is good	because	c) it is good for your health.
4	☐	Many people go to university		d) it is a world language.
5	☐	Taking exercise is important		e) you can shop from home.

Learning English is important because it is a world language.

3 Work with a partner. Link the sentences using *because*.

1 I like working in the library. It is quiet.
   I like working in the library because it is quiet.
2 I travel by car. I like driving.
3 I study biology and chemistry. I want to be a doctor.
4 I play squash and tennis. I like sport.
5 The course is interesting. The teachers are good.

4 Complete the sentences with information about you. Compare your sentences with a partner.

1 I like / don't like learning English because …
2 I go / don't go to the library because …
3 I like / don't like watching TV because …
4 I get up early / don't get up early because …
5 I study _____ (subject) because …

5 Work with a partner. Complete the text with words and phrases from the box.

a lot	evenings	law	lecture theatre	library	quiet

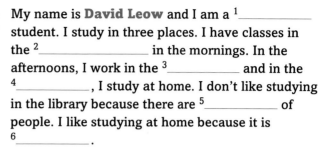

My name is **David Leow** and I am a ¹_____ student. I study in three places. I have classes in the ²_____ in the mornings. In the afternoons, I work in the ³_____ and in the ⁴_____, I study at home. I don't like studying in the library because there are ⁵_____ of people. I like studying at home because it is ⁶_____ .

6 Make notes about you in the chart.

1 Where do you study?
2 When do you study?
3 Which places do you like? Why?
4 Which places don't you like? Why not?

Where?	
When?	
Places I like	
Places I don't like	

7 Write a short paragraph about where you study. Use your notes from exercise 6. Link your ideas with *and*, *but*, and *because*.

My name is … and I am a … . I …

8 Work with a partner. Check your partner's work for mistakes in:

- grammar (articles, time prepositions, subject and verb agreement)
- punctuation (full stops, commas, capital letters)
- spelling
- linking words (*and*, *but*, *because*)

RESEARCH Search engines

1 Read STUDY SKILL Work with a partner.
   Underline the important words.

   1 <u>Where</u> is the <u>Euphrates</u>?
   2 Which countries border Thailand?
   3 What is the population of Japan?
   4 What does 'career' mean?
   5 What types of engineering are there?
   6 What is Karl Benz famous for?

> **STUDY SKILL** Using a search engine (1)
>
> Use a search engine on your computer, for example *Google* or *Yahoo*, to find
> information you need.
> - Choose important words (question words, nouns, and verbs).
> - Spell the words carefully.
> - Use 'define:' to find the meaning of the word. For example, *'define: profession'*.
> - Use first names and family names for people, for example *Alexander Bell*.

2 Write the underlined words from exercise 1 to put
   in a search engine. Check your answers with a partner.

   1 <u>where Euphrates</u>
   2 _____
   3 _____
   4 _____
   5 _____
   6 _____

3 Use a search engine on your computer to answer the questions in exercise 1.

VOCABULARY DEVELOPMENT Vocabulary records

1 Put the words into alphabetical order. Check your answers with a partner.

cheap	1 _____
drawing	2 _____
health	3 _____
spell	4 _____
know	5 _____
career	6 _____

2 Read STUDY SKILL Use a dictionary and make vocabulary
   records for three words in exercise 1.

> **STUDY SKILL** Recording vocabulary (2)
>
> It is important to keep a record of new vocabulary.
> Write the new words in a notebook or computer file. Write:
> - the word
> - the part of speech, e.g. noun, verb, adverb, adjective
> - the meaning
> - an example sentence
> - a translation

word	part of speech	meaning	example sentence	translation
career	noun	a job you learn to do and then do for years	Medicine is a good career.	carrière

3 Compare your records with a partner.

REVIEW

1 Look at the pictures. Who is the text about?

    a) doctors   b) engineers   c) teachers

An important job

Civil engineers do important work. They design and build bridges, roads, railways, and airports. Some of the time they work in offices. They use computers to plan their work. They can also work outside in a lot of different places, for example, in deserts, on the sea, and in our cities. Sometimes, working outside is difficult because of the weather. Civil engineers also work long hours and weekends, but they like their work because it is important and useful.

2 Skim the text and check your answer to exercise 1.

3 Underline the important words in the questions.

   1   What do civil engineers build?

   2   What do they use to plan their work?

   3   What are the three examples of outside work places?

   4   Why is working outside difficult?

   5   Why do civil engineers like their work?

4 Scan the text in exercise 1. Find and underline the important words from the questions in exercise 3.

5 Read the text and answer the questions in exercise 3.

6 Complete the text below with *and*, *but*, and *because*. Check your answers with a partner.

My name's Liu Yang, [1]_____ I'm a civil engineer. Civil engineering is a good career [2]_____ you can go to a lot of different places. I work in an office in the city most of the time, [3]_____ I also work outside on building sites sometimes. I like working in both places [4]_____ they are different. My office is clean [5]_____ quiet, [6]_____ the building site is dirty [7]_____ noisy.

5 Signs and instructions

READING SKILLS Understanding a text
WRITING SKILLS Completing a form
VOCABULARY DEVELOPMENT Recording vocabulary (3)

READING Signs – an international language

1 Work in small groups. Answer the questions.

   1 What signs are there in the streets in your town?
   2 What signs do you have in your university or college?

2 Read **STUDY SKILLS REVIEW** Work with a partner.
Survey the pictures and the text *Signs around the world*.
Answer the questions.

   1 What is the text about?
   2 What do the signs in pictures a–c mean?
   3 How many paragraphs are there in the text?

STUDY SKILLS REVIEW Understanding a text

Use different reading skills to get the information you
need from a text:

■ **surveying** (see Study Skill p4)
■ **predicting** (see Study Skill p10)
■ **skimming** (see Study Skill p16)
■ **scanning** (see Study Skill p23)

Signs around the world

Signs give us information or instructions. They have writing or
pictures on them. Today, many countries around the world use the
same signs.

It is important that these signs are easy and clear for everyone to
understand. There are rules about the shape and colour. A circle is
an instruction or order, for example 'no entry'. A triangle tells you
about a danger, for example 'large animals crossing the road'.
A rectangle gives you information, for example 'exit', or 'leave here'.
The colour of a sign is also important. For example, red is for
danger and green is for safety.

Signs are a kind of international language, and everyone can
understand them because they are the same in many countries.

a

b

c

3 Skim the text *Signs around the world*. Which topics does the text discuss?

  a) the size of signs   b) the colour of signs   c) the shape of signs

4 Read the questions and underline the important words.

   1 What does a circle mean?
   2 What does a triangle mean?
   3 What does a rectangle mean?
   4 What do the colours red and green mean?

5 Scan the text and answer the questions in exercise 4.

6 Work with a partner. Survey the notice below. What is it about?

a) a lecture   b) a library   c) a cafeteria

RULES

1 Do not bring your bags into the library.
   Leave them in the lockers.

2 Show your student ID card to the librarian.

3 Do not eat or drink in the library.

4 Do not smoke in the library.

5 Turn off your mobile phone.

6 Talk quietly.

7 Use a memory stick to save documents on
   the library computers.

7 Work with a partner. Look at the signs. What do they mean?

a [ ]   b [ ]   c [ ]

d [ ]   e [ ]

8 Skim the notice in exercise 6. Match signs a–e with rules 1–7.
Which rules do not have a sign?

9 Scan the notice and answer the questions.

1 Where do you leave your bags?
2 Who wants to see your student identity card?
3 Can you talk?
4 Why do you need a memory stick?

WRITING Forms

1 Read **STUDY SKILL** Match the words and short phrases 1–8 with the meanings a)–h).

STUDY SKILL Completing a form

To complete a form correctly, read and follow the instructions carefully. For example:

- Use CAPITAL LETTERS.
- Tick the box ☑.

Forms often use short phrases, not questions or sentences. For example:

- Place of birth (= Where were you born?)

1	g	First name(s)	a)	What is your nationality?
2	☐	Family name	b)	What do you do?
3	☐	Address	c)	Sign your name here.
4	☐	Date of birth	d)	Where do you live?
5	☐	Place of birth	e)	When were you born?
6	☐	Occupation	f)	Where were you born?
7	☐	Nationality	g)	What are your first name(s)?
8	☐	Signature	h)	What is your family name?

2 Complete the form about Hiroko with words and phrases from exercise 1. Compare your answers with a partner.

My name is Hiroko Sato. I am Japanese and I was born in Kyoto, in Japan, on 2nd September 1994. I'm a maths student. I live at 22, Victoria Road, Manchester.

Landing card for the UK
Please complete clearly in CAPITAL letters.

Family name	SATO
First name(s)	HIROKO
Date of birth	02.09.1994
1 _____	KYOTO, JAPAN
2 _____	STUDENT
3 _____	JAPANESE
Address in the UK	22 VICTORIA ROAD, MANCHESTER, M14 6AQ
4 _____	H.Sato

3 Work with a partner. Look at the completed form. Find three mistakes.

Tanbury Sports Club
Registration form

Tsc

Please use CAPITAL letters and black ink.

First name(s) Hiroko
Family name SATO
Date of birth 02.09.1994
Occupation STUDENT

Tick the sports you are interested in
Football ☐   Basketball ☒   Swimming ☐   Running ☐   Volleyball ☐

---

4 Complete the form with information about you.

Highfield University
Library Application Form

HU

Use black ink and CAPITAL letters.

First name _____
Family name _____
Date of birth _____
Address _____
  _____
  _____
Telephone number _____
Course title _____

Please tick
Year of study ☐ 1st year   ☐ 2nd year   ☐ 3rd year

---

5 Work with a partner. Check your partner's form.

VOCABULARY DEVELOPMENT Topic areas

1 ❘ Read STUDY SKILL ❘ Work with a partner.
Write the words from the box in the table.

| black | blue | circle | green | rectangle |
| ~~red~~ | square | triangle | white | |

colours	shapes
red	

STUDY SKILL Recording vocabulary (3)

You can record vocabulary by topic. For example:

People at university: Places:
  lecturer   *lab*
  student   *library*
  librarian   *multimedia centre*

Add to the topic groups in your notebooks when you learn new words.

2 Work with a partner. Add three words to each topic.
Use your own ideas.

subjects at university	geographical features
engineering	mountains
law	deserts
_____	_____
_____	_____
_____	_____

3 Put the words into two groups. Choose a heading for
each group. Compare your answers with a partner.

| basketball | bus | car | football | plane |
| running | swimming | taxi | train | volleyball |

4 In 60 seconds, write words for the topic 'jobs'.
Compare your answers with a partner.

Jobs
a doctor

REVIEW

1 Work with a partner. Survey the text below. What is it?

a) an advertisement   b) a notice   c) an essay

Fire action

If you hear the fire alarm, follow the instructions:

1 Stay calm.
2 Leave the building.
3 Do not run.
4 Do not use the lift.
5 Go to the assembly point.
6 Do not go back into the building until it is safe.

2 Look at the signs. What do they mean?

a   b   c

3 Skim the text in exercise 1. Match signs a–c with three of the instructions 1–6.

4 Scan the text. Answer the questions.

1 What does it tell you to do?
2 What does it tell you not to do?

5 Work with a partner. Ask questions and complete the form with information about your partner. Check your partner's form is correct.

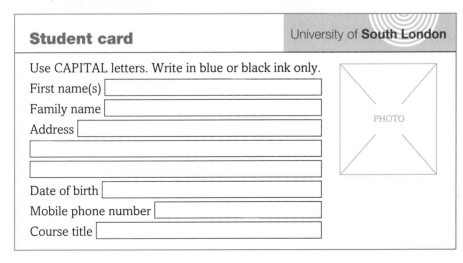

6 Health and medicine

READING Good health

1 Look at the photos. Work in small groups.
What do people do to stay healthy? Think about:

- sport
- food
- work / free time

2 Work with a partner. Survey the picture and text.
Answer the questions.

1 Where is the text from?
   a) a textbook
   b) an online encyclopedia
2 What does the picture show?
3 What is the text about?

Doing exercise

A fruit and vegetable market

Chapter 3 Health and hygiene

1 Health and hygiene are important all over the world today,
and they were important in the past. People from different
parts of the world made useful discoveries about health
and hygiene. These discoveries are still important today.

2 Medicine developed in the ancient world first. The
Egyptians made many medical discoveries. For example,
they used surgery to treat people. Later, the Greeks
thought a healthy life was important. They wanted people
to eat good food, to take exercise, and to sleep well. For
the Romans, hygiene was important. They built public
baths. They also had pipes to carry away dirty water
because it causes disease.

3 In the Middle East, medicine was also important. In
Baghdad, people built the first important hospital in the
world. It opened in 850 CE. Later, more hospitals opened
in the Middle East, and doctors studied medicine and
took exams.

4 Europeans used the information from these early doctors,
and made more developments in the next 1,000 years.
For example, in the 19th century, Florence Nightingale
saved many people's lives because she made hospitals
clean and safe.

5 Good public health today is a result of the work of people
from around the world. All these people in the past helped
it to develop and improve.

An Egyptian priest pouring medicine

145

3 Skim the text. Match topics a)–e) with paragraphs 1–5.

a) ☑2☑ Egyptians, Greeks, and Romans
b) ☐ the first hospital
c) ☐ public health today
d) ☐ a European woman
e) ☐ the importance of health and hygiene

4 Scan the text and answer the questions.

1 What three things did the Greeks want people to do?
2 What did the Romans build?
3 Where was the first important hospital?
4 What did Florence Nightingale do?

5 ▐ Read STUDY SKILL ▌ Look at the underlined pronouns in the text. Choose the noun that each pronoun replaces.

Paragraph 2

1 They
a) healthy life   b) the Greeks
c) international history

2 it
a) pipes   b) hygiene   c) dirty water

Paragraph 4

3 She
a) Florence Nightingale
b) hospitals
c) the 19th century

Paragraph 5

4 it
a) the world   b) public health   c) people

STUDY SKILL Understanding pronouns

Writers sometimes use pronouns, for example, *he, she, it, they*, in place of nouns, because they do not want to repeat the noun. For example:

- *Florence Nightingale*   ***she***
- *the Romans*   ***they***

The pronoun refers to a noun that comes before. For example,

- ***The Egyptians*** *made many medical discoveries.* ***They*** *used surgery to treat people.*

- *In Baghdad people built the first important* ***hospital*** *in the world.* ***It*** *opened in 850 CE.*

Understanding pronouns helps you understand a text.

---

6 Read the rules. Circle three regular Past Simple verbs and five irregular Past Simple verbs in paragraph 2 of the text.

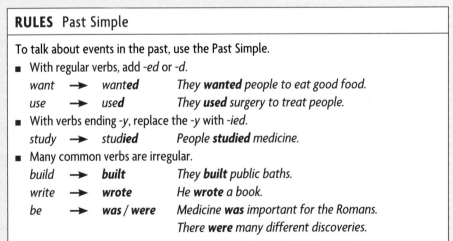

RULES Past Simple

To talk about events in the past, use the Past Simple.

- With regular verbs, add *-ed* or *-d*.

    want → want**ed**   They **wanted** people to eat good food.
    use   → us**ed**   They **used** surgery to treat people.

- With verbs ending *-y*, replace the *-y* with *-ied*.

    study → stud**ied**   People **studied** medicine.

- Many common verbs are irregular.

    build → **built**   They **built** public baths.
    write → **wrote**   He **wrote** a book.
    be   → **was / were** Medicine **was** important for the Romans.
                             There **were** many different discoveries.

WRITING Medical discoveries

1 Work with a partner. Look at the pair of sentences.
Is a) or b) better? Why?

a) In Baghdad, people built the first important hospital in the world.
It opened in 850 CE.

b) In Baghdad, people built the first important hospital in the world.
The first important hospital opened in 850 CE.

2 Read the rules. Underline the subject pronouns and circle the
object pronouns in the sentences.

1 <u>She</u> wrote many books. <u>She</u> wrote (them) in English.

2 I read about the Romans. They built many cities.

3 Jamil sent me an email. He wrote it on his phone.

4 Please give us your address.

5 They told her about the lecture.

RULES Pronouns						
Use **subject** and **object** pronouns in place of nouns.						
Subject pronouns	*I*	*you*	*he*	*she*	*it*	*we*	*they*
Object pronouns	*me*	*you*	*him*	*her*	*it*	*us*	*them*

3 **Read STUDY SKILL** Work with a partner. Complete the
sentences with a subject pronoun from the rules box.

1 Health was important for the Egyptians. _____
used surgery to treat diseases.

2 John is a scientist. _____ does research at a
hospital.

3 We read an article on the Internet. _____ was
very interesting.

4 My sister is a dentist. _____ works in the city.

5 My brother and I are medical students. _____ study at the
same university.

4 Complete the sentences with an object pronoun from the rules box.

1 Paul finished his homework yesterday and gave _____ to the
teacher this morning.

2 The student read about the Greeks and he wrote an essay about
_____ .

3 Anna is a medical researcher. I met _____ at a conference.

4 We saw Adam yesterday. We spoke to _____ after the lecture.

5 I didn't go to the lecture. Could you give _____ your notes,
please?

An early doctor seeing a patient

STUDY SKILL Avoiding repetition
We use pronouns to avoid repeating a noun. For example:
■ *Florence Nightingale worked in hospitals.*
~~*Florence Nightingale*~~ ***She*** *made* ~~*hospitals*~~ ***them*** *clean and safe.*
Use pronouns to improve your writing.

A medical researcher

5 Read the paragraph. Are the underlined words subjects (S) or objects (O)? Compare your answers with a partner.

Aspirin

Aspirin has a long history. Many years ago the Greeks discovered an important tree. <u>The Greeks</u> used <u>the tree</u> to make a medicine. The medicine stopped pain. Years later, scientists studied the medicine and <u>the scientists</u> called <u>the medicine</u> 'Aspirin'. People use <u>Aspirin</u> today to stop pain.

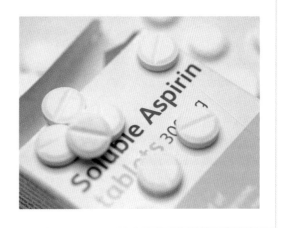

6 Replace the underlined words in exercise 5 with the correct pronouns.

7 Rewrite the student's paragraph. Use pronouns to avoid repetition.

A British woman, Mary Montagu, lived in Turkey in the eighteenth century. Mary Montagu had two children. Her children got ill. Mary took her children to see a Turkish doctor. The doctor helped the children. Mary went back to Britain. Mary told people about the Turkish doctor. Years later, a British doctor used the Turkish doctor's ideas to make a medicine. The medicine was the first vaccine. Vaccines stop people getting ill.

8 Compare your answers with a partner. Answer the questions.
  1 How many subject pronouns did you use?
  2 How many object pronouns did you use?

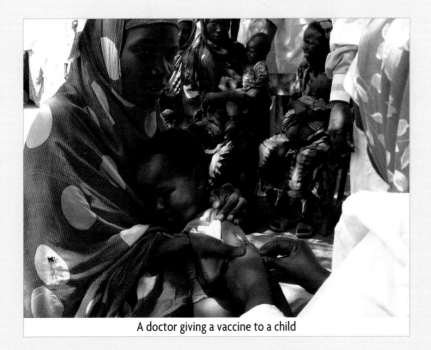

A doctor giving a vaccine to a child

VOCABULARY DEVELOPMENT Nouns and verbs

1 **Read STUDY SKILL** Are the underlined words in each pair of sentences nouns or verbs?

1 a) Did she <u>answer</u> the question?
   b) Did she know the <u>answer</u>?

2 a) My father is a <u>teacher</u>.
   b) He <u>teaches</u> at a university.

3 a) What did he <u>discover</u>?
   b) He made an important <u>discovery</u>.

STUDY SKILL Recognizing parts of speech

Some verbs and nouns are related.
Some nouns have the same form as the verb.

- *to circle*   *a circle*

Some nouns have a similar form to the verb, but have a noun ending.

- *to end*   *end**ing***
- *to teach*   *teach**er***
- *to introduce*   *introduc**tion***

Some verbs have more than one noun.

- *to begin*   *a begin**ner*** (the person)   *the begin**ning*** (the activity)

Making a note of nouns and verbs increases your vocabulary.

---

2 Work with a partner. Use a dictionary to find one or more nouns for each verb. Underline the noun endings.

verbs	nouns	
1 email	email	
2 introduce		
3 educate		
4 meet		
5 discuss		
6 lecture		
7 write		

3 Look at the sentences. Are the missing words verbs or nouns?

1 [noun] The scientist made an important d_____ .
2 [____] Dr Singh t_____ maths at the university.
3 [____] Send me an e_____ if you have any questions.
4 [____] We can discuss this at the m_____ tomorrow.
5 [____] It's important for students to get a good e_____ .

4 Complete the sentences in exercise 3 with words from exercises 1 and 2.

5 Work with a partner. Write sentences using the words in the box.

introduce   introduction   mean   meaning   write   writer

I'd like to introduce you to Dr Ahmed.

begin
*begin**ner***
*begin**ning***

teach
*teach**er***

REVIEW

1 Work with a partner. Survey the photo and the text. Answer the questions.

  1 What does the photo show?
  2 Where does the text come from?

2 Skim the text. Match topics a)–c) to paragraphs 1–3.

  a) ☐ chemicals in our food
  b) ☐ chemicals to stop malaria
  c) ☐ the importance of chemicals

Quinine leaves and bark

www.science-encyclopedia.com		Search

Chemicals and health

1 Many chemicals are important for our health. People started using chemicals years ago. <u>They</u> keep us healthy in different ways.

2 In tropical countries, malaria is a serious problem. People had <u>it</u> more than 4,000 years ago. In South America, people used a substance from a tree to treat malaria. They called it quinine. In China, they used a substance called artemisinin. Both quinine and artemisinin helped stop malaria, and people still use <u>them</u> today.

3 Food also stops disease. In the past, scientists studied food and its effect on disease. In 1912, a Polish scientist, Casimir Funk, did experiments on fruit and a type of rice. <u>He</u> found some chemicals in the food, and he called them vitamins. Vitamins are necessary in our food because they keep us healthy.

3 Work with a partner. Scan the text and answer the questions.

  1 Where is malaria a serious problem?
  2 Where does quinine come from?
  3 Why do people use quinine?
  4 What did Casimir Funk call the chemicals in food?
  5 Why are they important?

4 Look at the underlined pronouns in the text. Choose the noun that each pronoun replaces.

Paragraph 1	1 They	a) people	b) chemicals	c) years
Paragraph 2	2 it	a) people	b) tropical countries	c) malaria
	3 them	a) people	b) malaria	c) quinine and artemisin
Paragraph 3	4 He	a) food	b) diseases	c) a Polish scientist

5 Rewrite the student's paragraph. Use pronouns to avoid repetition.

> Another scientist did an experiment with food and disease in the 18th century. For a long time, sailors on boats got ill on long trips because sailors had no fruit and vegetables at sea. In 1747 an English doctor, James Lind, decided to do an experiment on sailors. James Lind gave the sailors lemon juice, and the sailors stayed healthy at sea. The lemon juice had vitamin C in it. Vitamin C is good for our skin and bones and keeps us healthy.

6 Work with a partner. Compare your answers.

  1 How many subject pronouns did you use?
  2 How many object pronouns did you use?

7 The history of transport

READING SKILLS Making notes (1)
KEY LANGUAGE Ordinal numbers • Dates
WRITING SKILLS Writing from notes
VOCABULARY DEVELOPMENT Using a dictionary (2) • Recording vocabulary (4)

READING Important first flights

1 Work in small groups. Answer the questions.

1 What do scientists do in space?
2 Is space research a good thing?
3 Would you like to travel in space? Why (not)?

2 Work with a partner. Survey the photos and text. Answer the questions.

1 What do the photos show?
2 What is the title?
3 How many paragraphs are there?
4 What is the text about?

a

Three steps into space

1 Three people, Yuri Gagarin, Valentina Tereshkova, and Neil Armstrong, all achieved important firsts in space.

2 Yuri Gagarin, a Russian, was always interested in space. He learned to fly at college, and in 1960 he became a pilot. A year later, on 12th April 1961, he was the first person to travel into space, in the spaceship Vostok.

3 Two years later, a young Russian, Valentina Tereshkova, became the first woman in space. Tereshkova was a twenty-six year old factory worker. Then she joined the Russian space programme, and on 16th June 1963 she left Earth in Vostok 6.

4 Six years later, three Americans left Earth in Apollo 11. On 20th July 1969, they landed on the moon. Neil Armstrong left the spaceship and became the first person to walk on the moon.

b

3 Skim the text. Match photos a–c with paragraphs 2–4.

4 Scan the text. Complete the sentences with the correct number or date. Check your answers with a partner.

1 Gagarin became a pilot in _____ .
2 He went into space on _____ April _____ .
3 Tereshkova left Earth on _____ June _____ .
4 She travelled in Vostok _____ .
5 _____ years later, the Americans left Earth in Apollo _____ .
6 Apollo _____ landed on the moon on 20th July _____ .

c

5 **Read STUDY SKILL** Read the text on page 40 again and complete the notes in the table. Compare your answers with a partner.

name	Yuri Gagarin		
nationality			American
spaceship		Vostok 6	
date	12th April 1961		
first			

STUDY SKILL Making notes (1)

When you read, make notes of useful information. Look for:
- important words
- names
- numbers and dates

6 Survey the photos and the text below. What is the text about?

a ☐

The Kitty Hawk

b ☐

Cornu's helicopter

c ☐

The Montgolfier balloon

1 In the history of flying, there are three important inventions, the hot-air balloon, the plane, and the helicopter.

2 In the eighteenth century, the Montgolfier brothers from France designed and made a hot-air balloon. The first flight with people was on the 21st November 1783. The balloon flew for four minutes.

3 Two American brothers, Orville and Wilbur Wright, designed and built a plane. They called it the Kitty Hawk. On the 17th December 1903, they flew the plane for the first time. They flew for 12 seconds.

4 Four years later, another Frenchman, Paul Cornu, built a helicopter. On the 13th November 1907, Cornu left the ground in his helicopter and flew for 20 seconds.

7 Skim the text. Match photos a–c with paragraphs 2–4.

8 Read the text. Complete the notes in the table. Compare your answers with a partner.

inventions	hot-air balloon		
inventors			
nationality		American	
date of first flight			
time of first flight			20 seconds

KEY LANGUAGE Ordinal numbers

1 Read STUDY SKILL Write the words in the box next to the ordinal numbers.

eighth	fifth	~~first~~	fourth	ninth	second
seventh	sixth	tenth	third		

1st	_first_	6th	_____
2nd	_____	7th	_____
3rd	_____	8th	_____
4th	_____	9th	_____
5th	_____	10th	_____

> **STUDY SKILL** Ordinal numbers
>
> Ordinal numbers are used for:
> - dates, for example *7th September*
> - centuries (= 100 years), for example *19th century* (= from 1800 to 1899)
> - the order of something, for example *first, second, third*
>
> It is important to understand how to read and write them.
>
> *1 first 1st   2 second 2nd   3 third 3rd*
>
> Most other ordinal numbers use *th*. For example:
> *4 fourth 4th,   5 fifth 5th*

2 Write the words as ordinal numbers. Check your answers with a partner.

1 eighteen   _18th_
2 nineteenth   _____
3 twentieth   _____
4 twenty-first _____
5 twenty-third _____

3 Match years 1–4 with centuries a)–d).

1 ☐ 1969   a) 21st century
2 ☐ 1783   b) nineteenth century
3 ☐ 2001   c) 20th century
4 ☐ 1830   d) eighteenth century

4 In 60 seconds, answer the questions. Compare your answers with a partner.

1 What is the 12th letter of the alphabet?
2 What is the 3rd letter of the alphabet?
3 What is the 24th letter of the alphabet?
4 What is the 16th letter of the alphabet?
5 What is the 20th letter of the alphabet?

Dates

5 Write the months of the year in the correct order.

January,

April	August	December	February	~~January~~	July
June	March	May	November	October	September

Compare your answers with a partner.

6 Read STUDY SKILL Write the dates. Use an ordinal number, the name of the month, and the year.

a) 11/10/2012   *11th October 2012*   c) 21/2/2011
b) 30/11/2010   d) 23/4/2013

> **STUDY SKILL** Dates
>
> Dates in British English are written:
> day / month / year
>
> In academic writing, use ordinals and the name of the month:
> - *26th February 2011*
>
> In notes, use numbers:
> - *26/2/2011*
>
> Start days of the week and months of the year with a capital letter.
> - *Monday, Tuesday, January, February*

7 Write the following dates in two ways:

	notes	academic writing
1 your date of birth	_____	_____
2 an important date for your country	_____	_____
3 an important date for your family	_____	_____

WRITING Trains

1 Label the photos with the words in the box.

> passenger train   underground train

a _____

b _____

2 Skim paragraph 1 of the text below. What is the text about?

   a) the speed of trains   b) the price of trains   c) the history of trains

Railway firsts

1 There were two important developments in railway history in England in the nineteenth century. One was the development of a long-distance train service for people. The second development was the introduction of the first underground train service.

2 The first long-distance train service started on 15th September 1830. It went a distance of 56 kilometres from Liverpool to Manchester. The engineer was George Stephenson. After a few weeks, it was very successful and carried thousands of people.

3 The other development was the first …

---

3 **Read STUDY SKILL** Read paragraph 2 of the text. Number the notes 1–5 in the order they are in the text.

date	15/09/1830	☐
where	Liverpool to Manchester	☐
what	first long-distance passenger train	☑ 1
engineer	George Stephenson	☐
distance	56 km	☐

> **STUDY SKILL** Writing from notes
>
> When you are writing from your notes:
> - Decide what the first point, and what the second point is.
> - Number your notes.
> - Write your text in order.

4 Read the notes for paragraph 3 of the text. Decide the order of the notes 1–5. Compare your ideas with a partner.

where	London	☐
distance	6.2 km	☐
engineer	John Fowler	☐
date	10/01/1863	☐
what	first underground train	☑ 1

5 Write paragraph 3 of the text about railway firsts. Use the notes in your order 1–5 in exercise 4.

6 Work with a partner. Check your partner's paragraph for mistakes with:

- dates
- verbs and prepositions
- punctuation (capital letters, commas, full stops)

VOCABULARY DEVELOPMENT Verbs in the Past Simple

1 Work with a partner. Write the regular and irregular verbs in the table.

arrived became
called   did
learned   left
paid   started
travelled   went

regular	irregular
arrived	became

2 Read STUDY SKILL Use a dictionary to find the Past Simple of the verbs. Compare your answers with a partner.

1 begin _began_
2 teach _____
3 see _____
4 drive _____
5 know _____

3 Complete the sentences with the verb in brackets in the Past Simple. Use a dictionary to help.

1 The teacher _____ (write) the new words on the board.
2 My tutor _____ (send) me an email about my homework.
3 I _____ (have) an English exam yesterday.
4 We _____ (read) a story in English in class.
5 Yousef and I _____ (do) the exercise together.

Verb + preposition

4 Work with a partner. Circle the correct preposition. Use a dictionary to help.

1 Work *with* / *by* a partner.
2 Look *in* / *at* the board.
3 Listen *to* / *of* your partner's presentation.
4 Turn *in* / *to* page 60.
5 Ask *for* / *from* help if you don't understand.
6 Talk *in* / *to* your partners and ask them the questions.

5 Work with a partner. Complete the sentences with the correct prepositions. Use a dictionary to help.

1 My homework is to write _____ the history of ships.
2 Yesterday we talked _____ the history of transport.
3 Last night I prepared _____ the maths test.
4 That bag belongs _____ Professor Lopez.
5 Give your essay _____ your teacher.

6 Read STUDY SKILL Make a vocabulary record for the verbs and prepositions below. Write your own example sentences.

1 come from   2 look for   3 talk about   4 arrive in

come from   verb + prep   Past: came from
+ place/country of birth   Example: I come from Rio de Janeiro

---

STUDY SKILL Using a dictionary (2)

- Good dictionaries give the irregular forms of verbs.
- Many dictionaries also have a list of irregular verbs.
- Use a dictionary (book, online, electronic) to check the spelling of the Past Simple of verbs.

begin 0━ /brˈgɪn/ *verb* (begins, beginning, began /brˈgæn/, has begun /brˈgʌn/)
1 to start to do something or start to happen ⊃ SAME MEANING **start**: *I'm beginning to feel cold.* ◇ *The film begins at 7.30.*
2 to start in a particular way: *The name John begins with a 'J'.* ⊃ OPPOSITE **end**
to begin with at first; at the beginning: *To begin with they were very happy.*

🔎 WHICH WORD?
Begin or **start**?
Begin and **start** both mean the same thing, but **start** is more often used in speaking: *Shall we eat now? I'm starting to feel hungry.*

Definitions from the Oxford Essential Dictionary © Oxford University Press

Infinitive	Past tense	Past participle
beat	beat	beaten
become	became	become
begin	began	begun

STUDY SKILL Recording vocabulary (4)

To help you use a verb correctly, record the prepositions that follow it. Write example sentences for the verb and each of its prepositions. For example:

write
- *I **wrote** an email **to** my teacher.*
- *I **wrote about** electric trains for my homework.*

REVIEW

1 Survey the pictures from a text.
Is the text about …?

a) sailing in the Mediterranean
b) sailing across the Atlantic
c) sailing around the world

2 Skim the text. Match the person in the photo with one of the paragraphs 2–4.

Sailing firsts

1 Who was the first person to sail around the world? We don't know for sure, but in the history of round-the-world sailing, three people achieved important firsts.

2 Francis Chichester, from England, was a great sailor. On 27th August 1966, he sailed his boat *Gypsy Moth* around the world. He returned to England on 28th May 1967 after 226 days sailing. He was the first person to sail single-handed around the world from west to east.

3 Twenty-one years later, Kay Cottee became the first woman to sail around the world without stopping. Kay, an Australian, left her country on 29th November 1987 in her boat *First Lady*, and returned to Sydney on 5th June 1988. She was at sea for 189 days.

4 Another Australian, David Dicks, also achieved an important first. He became the youngest person to sail non-stop around the world. In February 1996, at the age of seventeen, David left Australia in his boat, *Seaflight*. He returned to Australia in November 1996, after nine months at sea.

3 Read the text. Complete the notes in the table.
Compare your answers with a partner.

who	what	when	how long	name of boat
Francis Chichester				
		29/11/87 – 5/6/88		
	youngest person to sail around world non-stop		9 months	

4 Read the notes for a paragraph about important firsts in car racing.
Number the notes 1–3.

	what	where	when	winning car	speed km/h
	1st Formula 1 grand prix (take place)	Silverstone, England	13/5/1950	Alfa Romeo (win)	(be) 146
	1st car race (be)	France	22/7/1894	Peugeot (win)	(be)19
	1st 'grand prix' race (be)	Le Mans, France	27/6/1906	Renault (win)	(be) 101

5 Write a paragraph about car racing. Use the notes in exercise 4.
Use the verbs in brackets.

Title: **Car racing: some important firsts**
The first car race was in France on 22nd July 1894. A Peugeot won the race. Its speed was 19 km/h.

6 Check your paragraph for mistakes with:

- dates
- verbs and prepositions
- punctuation (capital letters, commas, full stops)

8 Doing business

READING SKILLS Making notes (2)
WRITING SKILLS Writing polite emails
VOCABULARY DEVELOPMENT Using a dictionary (3)

READING The business of sport

1 Work in small groups. Answer the questions.

1 Are there big sports competitions in your country? Which sports?
2 Why do countries have big sports competitions?
3 Why do business students study sports?

2 Skim the emails. Which email asks the students to …?

a) prepare a talk
b) read some texts and make notes

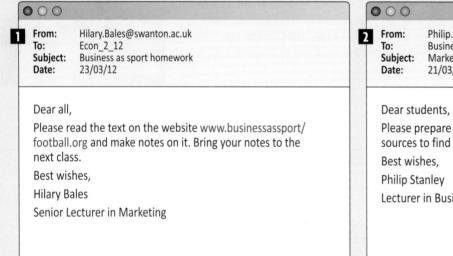

1
From:	Hilary.Bales@swanton.ac.uk
To:	Econ_2_12
Subject:	Business as sport homework
Date:	23/03/12

Dear all,

Please read the text on the website www.businessassport/football.org and make notes on it. Bring your notes to the next class.

Best wishes,

Hilary Bales

Senior Lecturer in Marketing

2
From:	Philip.Stanley@swanton.ac.uk
To:	Business Studies Group 4B
Subject:	Marketing course
Date:	21/03/12

Dear students,

Please prepare a short talk on online marketing. Use different sources to find your information. The talk is for next week.

Best wishes,

Philip Stanley

Lecturer in Business Studies

3 Work with a partner. Survey the webpage *The Business of Sport* on page 47. What is it about?

4 ▉Read STUDY SKILL▉ Skim the webpage. Match headings a)–e) with paragraphs 1–7. Which two paragraphs do not have a heading?

a) ☐ Money from TV
b) ☐ The business of football
c) ☐ Selling players
d) ☐ Advertising
e) ☐ Conclusion

> ### STUDY SKILL Making notes (2)
>
> To make notes:
> - Skim the text and write a heading for each paragraph.
> - Scan each paragraph and underline the most important words.
> - Write the underlined words under the paragraph headings.

5 Work with a partner. Choose the best headings for the other two paragraphs.

☐ Selling tickets ☐ Football on TV ☐ Selling products ☐ Football shirts

6 Write all the headings above the correct paragraphs on the web page.

The Business of Sport

1 [ ]

Today, sport is a business, and football is a good example. Football clubs need money to pay the players. There are five ways for the clubs to make money.

2 [ ]

Firstly, clubs sell tickets for the matches. A ticket for a match can be very expensive. The clubs also sell season tickets. These are tickets for all the matches in one year.

3 [ ]

Secondly, companies pay clubs to advertise. For example, there are signs for their products at the stadium and their logo is on the players' shirts.

4 [ ]

Some clubs make money from TV companies. This is usually only the big clubs, but it can be a lot of money for them.

5 [ ]

Clubs also sell products, for example, football shirts or hats. They sell their products in their shops and on the Internet. A lot of people buy them.

6 [ ]

Finally, a football club can sell a player to another club for a lot of money. Clubs can only do this twice a year.

7 [ ]

All clubs do these things, but only the top clubs get rich from them. Other sports also have to make money and they use the same ways.

7 Scan the text and underline the important words in each paragraph.

8 Make notes. Write the heading and important words for each paragraph. Compare your answers with a partner.

The business of football
clubs need money – pay players
5 ways

9 Use your notes in exercise 8 to answer the questions.
1 How many ways do football clubs make money?
2 What is the name for a ticket for all the matches in a year?
3 How do companies advertise at a football club?
4 What do clubs sell on the Internet?
5 What can clubs do twice a year?

WRITING Polite emails

1 Skim the emails and answer the questions.

　1 Who are the emails to?
　2 Who are they from?
　3 Which one is polite?

From: jack.carter@tmail.com
To: diana.stuart@wellington.ac.nz
Subject: the effect of money on sport
Date: 12.10.2012

Hello,

Here is my homework. Sorry I didn't go to your lecture yesterday. I was ill. Can you send me the handouts? Also, I want to talk to you about my studies.

Email me.

Bye,

Jack Carter

b

From: ana.gonzalez@interclub.com
To: diana.stuart@wellington.ac.nz
Subject: the effect of money on sport
Date: 12.10.2012

Dear Dr Stuart,

Please find attached my homework.

I am sorry that I missed your lecture yesterday on 'The effect of money on sport'. I was ill. Please could you send me the handouts? Also, I would like to talk to you about my studies.

I look forward to hearing from you.

Best wishes,

Ana Gonzalez

2 Scan email **b** and answer the questions.

　1 Did Ana do her homework?
　2 When was the lecture?
　3 What was the lecture on?
　4 Why didn't Ana go to the lecture?
　5 What does she want the lecturer to send her?

3 Look at these phrases from email **a**. Read email **b** and underline the polite phrases with the same meanings.

　1 Hello
　2 Here is my homework.
　3 Sorry I didn't go to your lecture.
　4 Can you send me the handouts?
　5 I want to talk to you.
　6 Email me.
　7 Bye

4 **Read STUDY SKILL** Match polite phrases 1–5 with endings a)–e) to make polite sentences.

1 ☐ Please could	a) my essay.
2 ☐ I am sorry that	b) we meet tomorrow?
3 ☐ Please find attached	c) talk to you about the course.
4 ☐ I look forward to	d) it is late.
5 ☐ I would like to	e) meeting you next week.

STUDY SKILL Writing polite emails

Learn and use polite phrases to write emails. For example:

- ***Dear*** *Dr Stuart*
- ***Please find attached*** *the PowerPoint for my presentation.*
- ***I am sorry that*** *it is late.*
- ***Please could you*** *send me the handouts?*
- ***I would like to*** *talk to you about my essay.*
- ***I look forward to*** *seeing you tomorrow.*
- ***Best wishes***, *Ana Gonzalez*

5 Read the email from Dr Brown. What does she want students to do?

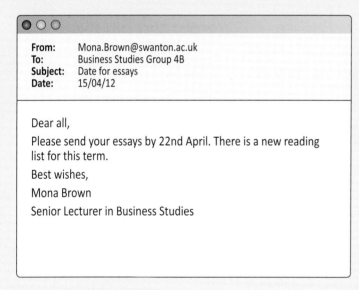

From: Mona.Brown@swanton.ac.uk
To: Business Studies Group 4B
Subject: Date for essays
Date: 15/04/12

Dear all,

Please send your essays by 22nd April. There is a new reading list for this term.

Best wishes,

Mona Brown

Senior Lecturer in Business Studies

6 Write an email to Dr Brown.

- Start the email correctly.
- Say that you are attaching your essay.
- Say it is late and you are sorry.
- Say you want a copy of the reading list.
- End the email correctly.

7 Work with a partner. Read your partner's email and check it for:

- polite phrases
- spelling
- capital letters
- punctuation

VOCABULARY DEVELOPMENT
Words with more than one meaning

1 | **Read STUDY SKILL** | Look at the pairs of sentences 1–4.
Write the part of speech for the underlined words.
Compare your answers with a partner.

	part of speech	meaning
1 a) Dr Stuart wrote a <u>book</u> about marketing.	_noun_	_1_
b) Did you <u>book</u> a room for the meeting?	___	___
2 a) The <u>table</u> shows the results of the study.	___	___
b) He left his computer on the <u>table</u>.	___	___
3 a) Connect the <u>mouse</u> to the computer.	___	___
b) A <u>mouse</u> ran across the floor.	___	___
4 a) Underline the <u>correct</u> answer.	___	___
b) The teacher is going to <u>correct</u> the exercise.	___	___

STUDY SKILL Using a dictionary (3)

Some words have more than one meaning.
For example, *kind* can be a noun or an
adjective with two different meanings.

- Look at all the entries for a word when
  you look it up in a dictionary.
- Choose the correct part of speech and
  meaning.

kind¹ 0⊸ /kaɪnd/ *noun*
a group of things or people that are the
same in some way ⊃ SAME MEANING **sort** or
type: *What kind of music do you like?* ◇ *The
shop sells ten different kinds of bread.*

kind² 0⊸ /kaɪnd/ *adjective* (kinder,
kindest)
friendly and good to other people: *'Can I
carry your bag?' 'Thanks. That's very kind of
you.'* ◇ *Be kind to animals.*
⊃ OPPOSITE **unkind**

2 Work with a partner. Look at the dictionary entries for the words in
exercise 1. Complete the table in exercise 1 with the number of the correct
meaning for each word.

book¹ 0⊸ /bʊk/ *noun*
a thing that you read or write in, that has a
lot of pieces of paper joined together inside
a cover: *I'm reading a **book** by George Orwell.*
◇ *an exercise book (= a book that you write in
at school)*

book² /bʊk/ *verb* (books, booking,
booked /bʊkt/)
to arrange to have or do something later: *We
booked a table for six at the restaurant.* ◇ *The
hotel is **fully booked** (= all the rooms are full).*

table 0⊸ /'teɪbl/ *noun*
1 a piece of furniture with a flat top on legs:
a coffee table ⊃ Look at Picture Dictionary
page **P10**.
2 a list of facts or numbers: *There is a **table** of
irregular verbs at the back of this dictionary.*

mouse 0⊸ /maʊs/ *noun* (*plural* mice
/maɪs/)
1 a small animal with a long tail: *Our cat
caught a mouse.*
2 a thing that you move with your hand to
tell a computer what to do

mice

correct¹ 0⊸ /kə'rekt/ *adjective*
right or true; with no mistakes: *What is the
correct time, please?* ◇ *All your answers were
correct.* ⊃ OPPOSITE **incorrect**
▶ **correctly** /kə'rektli/ *adverb*: *Have I spelt
your name correctly?*
⊃ OPPOSITE **incorrectly**

correct² 0⊸ /kə'rekt/ *verb* (corrects,
correcting, corrected)
to show where the mistakes are in
something and make it right: *The class did
the exercises and the teacher corrected them.* ◇
Please correct me if I make a mistake.

Definitions from the Oxford Essential Dictionary © Oxford University Press

3 Work with a partner. Use a dictionary to find two meanings for the words.
1 hard
2 virus
3 park
4 match

4 Write an example sentence for each meaning of the words in exercise 3.

REVIEW

1 Work with a partner. Survey the text and the picture. What is the text about?

Sports and television

1 [ ]

Television shows a lot of sports programmes. Sport on TV is a big business and many people benefit from it.

2 [ ]

When TV started in the 1940s, it showed sports. They were very popular because, for the first time, many people could watch important games. More people bought televisions and watched more sport.

3 [ ]

The TV companies paid the sports clubs and organizations a lot of money, and this is still true today. For example, in 1985 they paid $45 million to show the top basketball games in the USA. European TV companies paid 760 million euros to show the summer and winter Olympics of 2010 and 2012.

4 [ ]

How do the TV companies make money from sport? They sell time on television to other companies. These companies advertise their products at sports matches and competitions. Millions of people watch the sport and see the advertisements.

5 [ ]

Showing sports on TV has advantages for the top sports clubs and TV companies. Also, people around the world can watch their favourite sports at home.

---

2 Skim the text. Match headings a)–b) with two of the paragraphs 1–5.

a) [ ] The business of sport and TV

b) [ ] How TV companies make money

3 Write headings for the other paragraphs. Write all the headings above the correct paragraphs in the text. Compare your answers with a partner.

4 Scan the text and underline the important words in each paragraph.

5 Make notes. Write the heading and important words for each paragraph.

6 Use your notes in exercise 5 to answer the questions.

   1 Why was TV popular with sports fans in the 1940s?
   2 Who makes money from sport on TV?
   3 How do TV companies make money from sport?
   4 Why do companies advertise at sports matches and competitions?

7 Write an email to your teacher.

   • Start the email correctly.
   • Say that you are sorry you did not go to his / her lecture last week.
   • Ask for the handouts from the lecture.
   • Say that you are attaching the homework on sport and TV.
   • End the email correctly.

8 Work with a partner. Read your partner's email and check it for:

   • polite phrases   • spelling   • capital letters   • punctuation

READING SKILLS Understanding tables and charts (1) and (2)
WRITING SKILLS Describing statistics
VOCABULARY DEVELOPMENT Recording vocabulary (5)

READING Using water

1 Work with a partner. What do you use water for? Make a list in 30 seconds.

2 **Read STUDY SKILL** Survey the table and answer the questions.

1 What is the title of the table?
2 What are the headings in the table?
3 How many products are there in the table?

STUDY SKILL Understanding tables and charts (1)

Tables and bar charts show statistics. They are often used to compare numbers. Look at:
■ the title
■ the headings and topics
■ the numbers
Use the tables and charts to help you understand a text.

Litres of water necessary to produce one kilo of food								
product	apples	potatoes	bread	sugar	rice	chicken	beef	chocolate
litres of water	700	900	1,800	1,800	2,500	3,600	15,500	16,000

3 Scan the table and answer the questions.

1 How much water do we use to produce a kilo of potatoes?
2 Which product needs 3,600 litres of water?
3 Which product needs the most water?

4 Read the text and scan the table again. Correct mistakes 1–5 in the text.

Water for food

We need water to grow plants and to produce food. The table shows the number of litres of water necessary to produce [1]**seven** _eight_ kinds of food. The numbers are very different. For example, it takes [2]**900** _____ litres to produce a kilo of apples, but 15,500 litres for a kilo of [3]**chicken** _____. We use the same number of litres of water to produce a kilo of bread as a kilo of [4]**rice** _____. For chocolate it takes about [5]**26,000** _____ litres.

Why are these numbers so different? Some foods, such as beef and chocolate, use more water because they take a long time to produce.

5 Work with a partner. Survey the bar chart and answer the questions.
1 What is the title of the chart?
2 How many countries are there?

The use of water in different countries

Countries use water for three main reasons: in the home, for farming, and in industry. The bar chart shows the number of litres of water that people use in six countries. It is very different around the world. In the USA it is more than 550 litres a day, and in Australia the number is about the same as in the USA. In Japan it is 375 litres, and in China the number is less than in Japan, at 100 litres.

Water is cheap in many countries and we use a lot of it in our homes, but we use more to produce food and other goods.

There is a problem in many countries nowadays because we don't have much water. In the future, we need to find more, or use less.

Washing a car

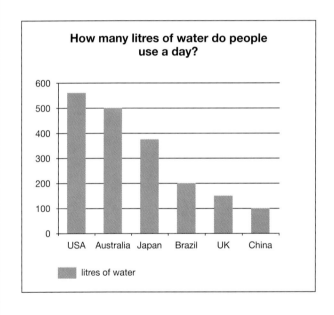

6 `Read STUDY SKILL` Read the text and scan the bar chart to answer the questions.
1 What are the three main uses of water?
2 How much water do people in Australia use?
3 Which country uses only 100 litres per day?
4 How much water do people in Brazil use?
5 Do we use more water in the home or in industry?
6 What is the problem in many countries?
7 What do we need to do?

STUDY SKILL Understanding tables and charts (2)

When you read a table or bar chart:
■ use a pencil or your finger to help you read the numbers.
■ check the numbers in the text with the table or bar chart.

WRITING More or less

1 Read STUDY SKILL Look at the pictures and write sentences. Use the phrases *more than / less than / the same as*. Compare your answers with a partner.

> **STUDY SKILL** Describing statistics
>
> Learn phrases to describe statistics. For example:
> - ***The bar chart shows*** the number of litres of water necessary to produce some food.
> - *In China the number is **less than** in Japan.*
> - *Some foods use **more** water because they take a long time to produce.*
> - *In Australia, the number is (about) **the same as** in the USA.*

1 people / Thailand / eat / more / rice / people / Japan
People in Thailand eat more rice than people in Japan.

2 people / Germany / eat / more / bread / people / the UK

3 people / Argentina / eat / less / fish / people / China

4 people / Pakistan / drink / the same number / cups of tea / people / India

2 Survey the table and answer the questions.
1 What is the title of the table?
2 What are the headings?

How many cups of coffee do people drink a day?	
country	**cups of coffee per day**
Finland	10
Germany	7
USA	5
Australia	2
Japan	2
Oman	1

3 Scan the table. Are the sentences true (**T**) or false (**F**)?

1 In Finland people drink less coffee than in Germany.
2 People drink more coffee in Germany than in the USA.
3 People in Australia and Japan drink the same amount of coffee.
4 People drink less coffee in Japan than in Oman.

4 Scan the table on page 54 again and complete the text below. Use the words in the box.

| as | less | more | more | same | shows | than |

Coffee around the world

Coffee is a very popular drink. The table ¹_____ how many cups of coffee people drink in a day. People drink ²_____ coffee in Finland ³_____ in other countries. They drink about ten cups a day.

In Australia people drink the ⁴_____ number ⁵_____ in Japan, but people in Oman drink ⁶_____ coffee, only one cup a day.

Do people drink ⁷_____ coffee in some countries because the weather is cold?

5 Survey the bar chart below and answer the questions.
1 What is the title?
2 How many countries are there?

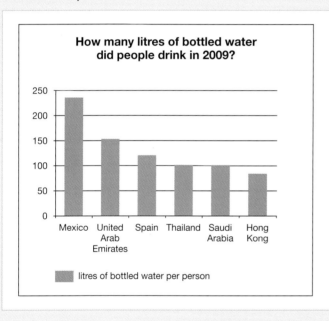

How many litres of bottled water did people drink in 2009?

litres of bottled water per person

6 Scan the bar chart and answer the questions.
1 Which country used more bottled water than the other countries?
2 How much bottled water did people drink in Spain?
3 Which two countries drank the same number of litres of bottled water?
4 Which country used less bottled water than the other countries?

7 Write a description of the bar chart. Use your answers in exercise 6.

The bar chart shows how many litres of bottled water people drank around the world in 2009. People in Mexico used ...

8 Work with a partner. Check your partner's writing for:
• spelling
• punctuation
• grammar

VOCABULARY DEVELOPMENT Opposite adjectives

1 Read STUDY SKILL Match adjectives 1–5 with their opposites a)–e).

1 ☐ wet		a) cold
2 ☐ noisy		b) long
3 ☐ short		c) bad
4 ☐ hot		d) quiet
5 ☐ good		e) dry

STUDY SKILL Recording vocabulary (5)

Many adjectives have an opposite. For example, the opposite of *large* is *small*.

Some adjectives use a prefix, such as *un* or *in*, to make an opposite. For example, *important* ≠ **un***important*.

Some adjectives have 2 opposites: a different word, and the same word with a prefix. For example, *expensive* ≠ **in***expensive*, *cheap*.

- Use your dictionary to find the opposite(s) of an adjective.
- Record adjectives with their opposite(s) to increase your vocabulary.

2 Work with a partner. Write the opposite of the adjectives from the box.

big	difficult	new	rich	right

1 easy _____
2 small _____
3 wrong _____
4 poor _____
5 old _____

big

small

old

new

3 Underline the adjectives in the sentences. Compare your answers with a partner.

1 In the 19th century, trains were very slow.
2 Juan is always late for class.
3 My email box is full.
4 Aminta always gets high marks in maths.

4 Work with a partner. Use a dictionary to find opposites for the adjectives in exercise 3.

5 Write the opposite of the adjectives using a prefix *un-* or *in-*. Use your dictionary to help.

1 important ___unimportant___
2 popular _____
3 dependent _____
4 complete _____
5 successful _____

6 Work with a partner. Use a dictionary to find two opposites for each adjective.

1 clean ___dirty___ ___unclean___
2 interesting _____ _____
3 safe _____ _____
4 healthy _____ _____
5 correct _____ _____

7 Work in small groups. Answer the questions.

1 Which subject at school was easy for you?
2 Which subject at school was difficult for you?
3 Where is a cheap place to eat in your town?
4 Where is an expensive place to eat?
5 Where is a quiet place to work?
6 Where is a noisy place to live?
7 What foods are healthy?
8 What foods are unhealthy?

REVIEW

1 Work with a partner. Look at the title of the text and the photo. What do you think the text is about?

a) drinking water   b) water sports   c) the oceans

2 Survey the table and answer the questions.

1 What is the title of the table?
2 What are the headings?
3 How many oceans are there in the table?

An important resource

The oceans cover about 70% of the world's surface and contain 97% of the Earth's water. There are five oceans, and they are all connected.

The table shows the size of the oceans. The Pacific Ocean is very big and covers an area of about 150 million square kilometres. The Atlantic Ocean is half the size of the Pacific Ocean and about the same size as the Indian Ocean. Scientists named the Southern Ocean for the first time in 2000. It surrounds Antarctica. The Arctic Ocean is quite small and very cold. It is covered by ice in the winter.

The oceans are very important. They give us a lot of our food, and some countries now change sea water into drinking water, too. We can also use oceans to transport goods, and we can find minerals in them. For all these reasons, we need to take care of the oceans and keep them clean.

The size of the oceans

ocean	size (million sq km)
Pacific	155
Atlantic	77
Indian	69
Southern	20
Arctic	14

3 Read the text and scan the table. Answer the questions.

1 How much of the Earth's water is in the oceans?
2 How big is the Atlantic Ocean?
3 When was the Southern Ocean named?
4 Which is the third ocean in size?
5 Which ocean is covered by ice in winter?
6 What do we use the oceans for?

4 The bar chart on the right shows the use of water in 1960 and 2010. Scan the bar chart and answer the questions.

1 In 1960, how much water did people use for:
a) agriculture?   b) industry?   c) the home?

2 In 2010, did people use more or less water than 1960 for:
a) agriculture?   b) industry?   c) the home?

3 Which figures in 1960 are about the same as the figures for 2010?

5 Use your answers in exercise 4 to write a description of the use of water in 1960 and 2010.

The bar chart shows the global use of water in 1960 and 2010. In 1960 ...

6 Work with a partner. Check your partner's writing for:

• spelling   • punctuation   • grammar

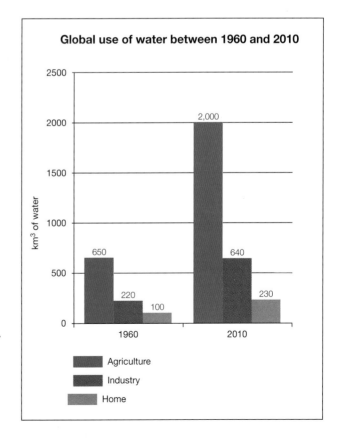

10 Ambition and success

READING SKILLS Understanding the organization of a text
WRITING SKILLS Writing a paragraph • Checking your writing (3)
RESEARCH Using a search engine (2) • Checking information

READING Great ideas

1 Work in small groups. Discuss the questions.

 1 Do you like shopping? Why (not)?
 2 Where do you shop?
 3 Do you shop on the Internet? Why (not)?
 4 What do people buy on the Internet?

2 Work with a partner. Survey the photos on page 59. Predict the topic of the text.

3 Skim the text. Were your ideas in exercise 2 correct?

4 **Read STUDY SKILL** Underline the first sentence in each paragraph in the text. Match headings a)–d) with paragraphs 1–4. Write the headings in the text.

a) ☐1 **An interesting start**
b) ☐ **Amazon today**
c) ☐ **Starting the business**
d) ☐ **A new idea**

> **STUDY SKILL** Understanding the organization of a text
>
> A topic sentence tells you what a paragraph is about. It is often the first sentence. Skim the text and underline the topic sentence in each paragraph. This helps you find information quickly.

5 Work with a partner. Decide which paragraph 1–4 has the answer to each question.

a) ☐ How many countries did he sell books to?
b) ☐ How rich is Bezos?
c) ☐ What did big companies use computer sciences to do?
d) ☐ What does Amazon sell now?
e) ☐ When did he open his online shop?
f) ☐ When did he have his new idea?
g) ☐ Where was Bezos born?
h) ☐ Which university did Bezos go to?

6 Go to the correct paragraph to answer the questions in exercise 5. Compare your answers with a partner.

A success story

Jeff Bezos

1 | An interesting start |

Jeff Bezos was born in the USA in 1964. When he was a child, he was very interested in science and computers. After school, he went to Princeton University. He planned to study physics, but changed to computer science and electrical engineering because he loved computers.

2 | |

In the early 1990s, Bezos had an idea for a new business. He worked for big companies on Wall Street in New York. He knew that these companies used computer sciences to study the business market. He also noticed that more and more people used the Internet every year for business, but not for ordinary shopping. So, after more research, he decided to start an online book shop.

Goods in a warehouse

3 | |

On 16th July 1995, Bezos started his new business. He opened his online shop from his garage. He called his business *Amazon*, and in one month he sold books in every state in the USA and in 45 different countries around the world. By September, it had $20,000 of sales every week.

4 | |

Today, Amazon.com is a huge success. It sells computer games, DVDs, electronics, and many other things, as well as books. In total, it sells more than 20 million different products. It has more than 10% of all online sales in the USA, and its creator, Jeff Bezos, is a billionaire.

Goods ready for delivery

WRITING Success

1 **Read STUDY SKILL** Sentences a)–f) are from a paragraph about Kiran Mazumdar-Shaw. Write number 1 next to the topic sentence and number 6 next to the final sentence.

a) ☐ At first, it was a very small company.

b) ☐ But she worked hard, and the company began to grow.

c) ☐ Kiran Mazumdar-Shaw is a successful businesswoman.

d) ☐ In 1978, she started a biotech company, *Biocon*, in a garage.

e) ☐ She was born in 1953 in Bangalore, in India.

f) ☐ Today, *Biocon* is one of the leading biotech companies in the world.

Kiran Mazumdar-Shaw

STUDY SKILL Writing a paragraph

A good paragraph is well-organized.

The topic sentence tells the reader what the paragraph is about.

Middle sentences are:
- on the same topic
- organized logically

The final sentence concludes the topic.

2 Look at the sentences in exercise 1 again. Number the middle sentences from 2 to 5. Compare your answers with a partner.

3 Use the notes below to write a paragraph about Tamara Mellon. Write full sentences in the same order as the headings. Start with the topic sentence.

Topic
Tamara Mellon – successful businesswoman

Early life
born England 1967
worked for Vogue (fashion magazine)

New idea
liked shoes
decided to sell expensive shoes

Start of company
opened 1st shop London 1996 with designer Jimmy Choo

Success
now – over 110 shops worldwide

Tamara Mellon

Tamara Mellon is a successful businesswoman. She ...

4 **Read STUDY SKILL** Read the student's paragraph. Find and correct:

- two punctuation mistakes
- two spelling mistakes
- one grammar mistake (article)
- one linking word mistake

Compare your answers with a partner.

STUDY SKILL Checking your writing (3)

Before you hand in an essay, it is important to check it. Look for mistakes in:

- punctuation, for example capital letters, full stops, commas
- spelling, for example irregular plural nouns, and Past Simple verbs
- grammar, for example subject and verb agreement, articles
- sentence structure, for example subject + verb + object
- linking words, for example *and*, *but*, *because*

> Sergey Brin and Larry Page co-founded Google in 1998. They met at Stanford University, but decided to look at search technologys, that is, how to find information on the Internet. This gave them a idea for a new company On 7th September 1998, they startd their business in a garage, like Jeff bezos. At first, it got about 10,000 searches a day, but now it gets over two billion.

5 Check your paragraph from exercise 3 on page 60 for mistakes.

RESEARCH Finding the right information

1 **Read STUDY SKILL** Work with a partner. You need to find out the information in 1–8. Look at the search engine screen and write where you can find the information. Write *Web*, *Images*, *Maps*, or *Translate*.

1 a photograph of Sebastian Vettel, the racing driver   *Images*
2 the countries that border Zambia
3 the word 'efficient' in your language
4 where Sabeer Bhatia was born
5 the capital city of Morocco
6 the date of the first supersonic flight by Concorde
7 where the shop 'Harrods' is in London
8 a picture of the Ferrari 458 Italia

STUDY SKILL Using a search engine (2)

Use a search engine to find different types of information. Go to:

- **Web** for facts, for example dates, capitals, names, etc.
- **Images** for photographs, pictures, etc.
- **Maps** for countries, cities, etc.
- **Translate** for changing a word from one language to another

2 Use a search engine to find the information in exercise 1. Compare your answers with a partner.

3 `Read STUDY SKILL` Read the information from websites 1 and 2. Find two differences.

> **1** www.jsmith.blogs.com `Search`
>
> ## Jack Smith's history of Hotmail
>
> Welcome to my history of Hotmail. Today, Hotmail is the world's largest email provider with 50 million users. Bhatia started the company in 1996 and sold it to Microsoft in 1998.

> **2** businet.com `Search`
>
> ## BUSINESS FORUM
>
> Hotmail is the world's largest web-based email service, with nearly 364 million users. Microsoft bought Hotmail in 1997.

STUDY SKILL Checking information

Some websites are open. This means that the information can be changed.

Other websites are business or personal sites. This means that the information is not always accurate. Always check your information on two or more websites.

4 Look at the information from website 3, an online encyclopedia. Compare the information with websites 1 and 2. Choose the correct answers a) or b).

1 When did Microsoft buy Hotmail?
   a) 1997   b) 1998

2 How many Hotmail users are there?
   a) 50 million people   b) more than 360 million people

> **3** longfordenc.ac.uk `Search`
>
> ### Longford Encyclopedia
>
> Microsoft bought Hotmail in 1997. Today it has hundreds of millions of users around the world.

5 Look at the headings for notes about Sabeer Bhatia. Number the headings in the order you will write about them.

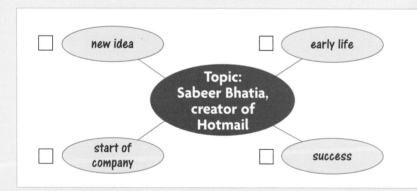

Sabeer Bhatia

6 Use a search engine to find two pieces of information to write under each heading.

7 Write a paragraph about Sabeer Bhatia. Use your notes from exercise 6. Remember to write:

- a topic sentence
- middle sentences in a logical order
- a final sentence

8 Check your work for mistakes.

REVIEW

1 Skim the text and underline the topic sentence in each paragraph.

2 Match headings a)–d) to the topic sentence of each paragraph 1–4. Write the headings in the text.
   a) ☐ **International success**
   b) ☐ **Learning**
   c) ☐ **Starting the business**
   d) ☐ **The businessman**

3 Read the questions. Which paragraph (1–4) has the answer to each question?
   a) ☐ How many people work for Superdry today?
   b) ☐ What did he do after school?
   c) ☐ What was his new idea?
   d) ☐ What parts of the world have Superdry shops?
   e) ☐ Where did he open his first shop?
   f) ☐ Why did Superdry become successful in 2005?
   g) ☐ Why didn't he go to university to study medicine?

4 Read the text and answer the questions in exercise 3.

5 Choose a successful person from your country. Use a search engine to find information about the person. Write notes about:
   • early life and education
   • career
   • achievements

6 Write a paragraph about the person from exercise 5.
   • Write a topic sentence.
   • Organize the middle sentences logically.
   • Write a final sentence.
   • Check your work for mistakes.

The story of Superdry

1 | The businessman |

Julian Dunkerton is a successful businessman. He is the founder of the clothing brand 'Superdry'. He was born in England in 1965. He wanted to be a doctor, but he did not get good exam results at school. So, when he left school, he did not go to university, but started selling clothes in a market.

Julian Dunkerton

2 | |

At the market, he learnt a lot about people. He learnt about what clothes they liked and what clothes they did not like. He realized that there were lots of people who wanted fashionable and cool clothes but did not want 'strange' clothing. He decided to design and sell clothes for these people.

3 | |

He started his new business with very little money. He called his business 'Cult Clothing'. But when he opened his first shop in London in 2004, he called it 'Superdry'. The company became very successful in 2005 because David Beckham, an English footballer, wore a Superdry T-shirt.

4 | |

Superdry today is a huge international success. It has shops in Europe, the Middle East, Asia, Australia, and the Americas, and it employs thousands of people. Julian Dunkerton started selling clothes in a market, but today he is a multi-millionaire.

WORD LIST

Here is a list of most of the new words in the units of *New Headway Academic Skills*, Introductory Level Student's Book.

adj = adjective
adv = adverb
conj = conjunction
n = noun
pl = plural
prep = preposition
v = verb

Unit 1

a lot of /ə 'lɒt əv/
about *prep* /ə'baʊt/
accountant *n* /ə'kaʊntənt/
add *v* /æd/
alphabet *n* /'ælfəbet/
alphabetical order *n* /ˌælfə'betɪkl 'ɔːdə(r)/
architect *n* /'ɑːkɪtekt/
article *n* /'ɑːtɪkl/
ask *v* /ɑːsk/
Australia *n* /ɒ'streɪlɪə/

backgammon *n* /'bækgæmən/
be *v* /biː/
before *prep* /bɪ'fɔː(r)/
beginner *n* /bɪ'gɪnə(r)/
below *prep* /bɪ'ləʊ/
book *n* /bʊk/
Brazil *n* /brə'zɪl/
brother *n* /'brʌðə(r)/
businesswoman *n* /'bɪznəswʊmən/

capital letters *n pl* /ˌkæpɪtl 'letəz/
carefully *adv* /'keəfəli/
check *v* /tʃek/
chess *n* /tʃes/
children *n pl* /'tʃɪldrən/
circle *v* /'sɜːkl/
city *n* /'sɪti/
club *n* /klʌb/
come from *v* /'kʌm frɒm/
complete *v* /kəm'pliːt/
computer engineering *n* /kəm'pjuːtə(r) ˌendʒɪ'nɪərɪŋ/
computer programmer *n* /kəm'pjuːtə 'prəʊgræmə(r)/
conference *n* /'kɒnfərəns/
consonants *n pl* /'kɒnsənənts/
correct (*v, adj*) /kə'rekt/
country *n* /'kʌntri/
course *n* /kɔːs/

daughter *n* /'dɔːtə(r)/
dentist *n* /'dentɪst/
dictionary *n* /'dɪkʃənri/
do *v* /duː/

doctor *n* /'dɒktə(r)/
end *v* /end/
engineer *n* /ˌendʒɪ'nɪə(r)/
English Language teacher *n* /'ɪŋglɪʃ 'læŋgwɪdʒ 'tiːtʃə(r)/
especially *adv* /ɪ'speʃəli/
family *n* /'fæməli/
father *n* /'fɑːðə(r)/
find *v* /faɪnd/
for example /fɔː(r) ɪg'zɑːmpl/
four /fɔː(r)/
friends *n pl* /frendz/
from *prep* /frɒm/
full stop *n* /ˌfʊl 'stɒp/

go *v* /gəʊ/

have *v* /hæv/
help *v* /help/
hospital *n* /'hɒspɪtl/
housewife *n* /'haʊswaɪf/
how many /haʊ 'meni/
husband *n* /'hʌzbənd/
important *adj* /ɪm'pɔːtnt/

in *prep* /ɪn/
index *n* /'ɪndeks/
India *n* /'ɪndɪə/
instructions *n pl* /ɪn'strʌkʃnz/
international school *n* /ˌɪntə'næʃnəl skuːl/
Internet *n* /'ɪntənet/
introductions *n pl* /ˌɪntrə'dʌkʃnz/

Japan *n* /dʒə'pæn/
keyboard *n* /'kiːbɔːd/
know *v* /nəʊ/

label *v* /'leɪbl/
learn *v* /lɜːn/
lecturer *n* /'lektʃərə(r)/
letters *n pl* /'letəz/
like *v* /laɪk/
live *v* /lɪv/
look at *v* /'lʊk æt/

make sure *v* /meɪk 'ʃɔː(r)/
married *adj* /'mærɪd/
match *v* /mætʃ/
medical student *n* /'medɪkl 'stjuːdnt/
meet *v* /miːt/
members *n pl* /'membəz/
men *n pl* /men/
mistake *n* /mɪ'steɪk/

name *n* /neɪm/
necessary *adj* /'nesəsəri/
new *adj* /njuː/
noun *n* /naʊn/
number *v* /'nʌmbə(r)/
nurse *n* /nɜːs/

occupation *n* /ˌɒkju'peɪʃn/
office *n* /'ɒfɪs/
one /wʌn/
online *adj* /ˌɒn'laɪn/

page *n* /peɪdʒ/

paragraph *n* /'pærəgrɑːf/
partner *n* /'pɑːtnə(r)/
people *n pl* /'piːpl/
Philippines *n* /'fɪlɪpiːnz/
photo *n* /'fəʊtəʊ/
picture *n* /'pɪktʃə(r)/
places *n pl* /pleɪsɪz/
play *v* /pleɪ/
punctuation *n* /ˌpʌŋktʃu'eɪʃn/
question *n* /'kwestʃən/
question mark *n* /'kwestʃən mɑːk/
quickly *adv* /'kwɪkli/

read *v* /riːd/
register *v* /'redʒɪstə(r)/
registration desk *n* /ˌredʒɪ'streɪʃn desk/
rules *n pl* /ruːlz/

screen *n* /skriːn/
sentence *n* /'sentəns/
sister *n* /'sɪstə(r)/
six /sɪks/
small letters *n pl* /smɔːl 'letəz/
son *n* /sʌn/
start *n* /stɑːt/
student *n* /'stjuːdnt/
study *v* /'stʌdi/
survey *v* /sə'veɪ/

text *n* /tekst/
textbook *n* /'tekstbʊk/
Thailand *n* /'taɪlænd/
title *n* /'taɪtl/
Turkey *v* /'tɜːki/
two /tuː/

uncle *n* /'ʌŋkl/
underline *v* /ˌʌndə'laɪn/
understand *v* /ˌʌndə'stænd/
university *n* /ˌjuːnɪ'vɜːsəti/
use *v* /juːz/

verb *n* /vɜːb/
very much *adv* /'veri mʌtʃ/
vowels *n pl* /'vaʊəlz/

webpage *n* /'webpeɪdʒ/
what? /wɒt/
where? /weə(r)/
which? /wɪtʃ/
with *prep* /wɪð/
word *n* /wɜːd/
work *v* /wɜːk/
write *v* /raɪt/

Unit 2

Africa *n* /'æfrɪkə/
agreement *n* /ə'griːmənt/
Algeria *n* /æl'dʒɪərɪə/
Algerian *adj* /æl'dʒɪərɪən/
along *prep* /ə'lɒŋ/
also *adv* /'ɔːlsəʊ/
Andorra *n* /æn'dɔːrə/
Angola *n* /æŋ'gəʊlə/
Arctic Ocean *n* /ˌɑːktɪk 'əʊʃn/
area *n* /'eərɪə/
Argentina *n* /ˌɑːdʒən'tiːnə/
around *prep* /ə'raʊnd/
Atlantic Ocean *n* /ətˌlæntɪk 'əʊʃn/

Bangladesh *n* /ˌbæŋglə'deʃ/
Bhutan *n* /buː'tɑːn/
big *adj* /bɪg/
Bolivia *n* /bə'lɪvɪə/
border *v* /'bɔːdə(r)/
borders *n pl* /'bɔːdəz/
Brunei *n* /bruː'naɪ/
Burma *n* /'bɜːmə/
but *conj* /bʌt/

Canada *n* /'kænədə/
capital (city) *n* /'kæpɪtl 'sɪti/
cars *n pl* /kɑːz/
centre *n* /'sentə(r)/
Chad *n* /tʃæd/
Chile *n* /'tʃɪli/
China *n* /'tʃaɪnə/
climate *n* /'klaɪmət/
coast *n* /kəʊst/
coastline *n* /'kəʊstlaɪn/
college *n* /'kɒlɪdʒ/
comma *n* /'kɒmə/

desert *n* /'dezət/
different *adj* /'dɪfrənt/
dry *adj* /draɪ/

easier *adj* /'iːzɪə(r)/
east *n* /iːst/
East Africa *n* /iːst 'æfrɪkə/
eight /eɪt/
Europe *n* /'jʊərəp/
example *n* /ɪg'zɑːmpl/
export *v* /ɪk'spɔːt/

five /faɪv/
flag *n* /flæg/
flat *adj* /flæt/
forest *n* /'fɒrɪst/
France *n* /frɑːns/

geography *n* /dʒi'ɒgrəfi/
grammar *n* /'græmə(r)/

half /hɑːf/
high *adj* /haɪ/
hill *n* /hɪl/
hot *adj* /hɒt/

idea *n* /aɪ'dɪə/
Indonesia *n* /ˌɪndə'niːʒə/
Italy *n* /'ɪtəli/

land *n* /lænd/
large *adj* /lɑːdʒ/
Libya *n* /'lɪbiə/
link *v* /lɪŋk/
list *n* /lɪst/
location *n* /ləʊ'keɪʃn/
long *adj* /lɒŋ/
Malaysia *n* /mə'leɪʒə/
Malaysian *adj* /mə'leɪʒn/
Mali *n* /'mɑːli/
many /'meni/
map *n* /mæp/
Mauretania *n* /ˌmɒrɪ'teɪniə/
meaning *n* /'miːnɪŋ/
medicines *n pl* /'medɪsnz/
Mediterranean Sea *n*
   /ˌmedɪtə'reɪniən siː/
Mexico *n* /'meksɪkəʊ/
million /'mɪljən/
modern *n* /'mɒdn/
Morocco *n* /mə'rɒkəʊ/
most /məʊst/
mountains *n pl* /'maʊntənz/
national *adj* /'næʃnəl/
Nepal *n* /nə'pɔːl/
New Zealand *n* /ˌnjuː 'ziːlənd/
Niger *n* /niː'ʒeə(r)/
north *n* /nɔːθ/
North Africa *n* /nɔːθ 'æfrɪkə/
North America *n* /nɔːθ ə'merɪkə/
Oceania *n* /əʊsi'ɑːniə/
oceans *n pl* /'əʊʃnz/
oil *n* /ɔɪl/
on *prep* /ɒn/
other *adj* /'ʌðə(r)/
over *prep* /'əʊvə(r)/
Pacific Ocean *n* /pəˌsɪfɪk 'əʊʃn/
Pakistan *n* /ˌpækɪ'stæn/
Paraguay *n* /'pærəgwaɪ/
part of speech *n* /ˌpɑːt əv 'spiːtʃ/
population *n* /ˌpɒpju'leɪʃn/
Portugal *n* /'pɔːtʃʊgl/
predict *v* /prɪ'dɪkt/
prepare *v* /prɪ'peə(r)/
rainforest *n* /'reɪnfɒrɪst/
river *n* /'rɪvə(r)/
Saudi Arabia *n* /ˌsaʊdi ə'reɪbiə/
school *n* /skuːl/
seas *n pl* /siːz/
second /'sekənd/
short *adj* /ʃɔːt/
similar *adj* /'sɪmələ(r)/
south *n* /saʊθ/
South Africa *n* /saʊθ'æfrɪkə/
South China Sea *n*
   /saʊθ 'tʃaɪnə siː/
South East Asia *n* /saʊθ iːst 'eɪʃə/
Spain *n* /speɪn/
state capital *n* /steɪt 'kæpɪtl/
Strait of Malacca *n*
   /streɪt ɒv mə'lakə/
subject *n* /'sʌbdʒekt/
sunny *adj* /'sʌni/
Switzerland *n* /'swɪtsələnd/
technical institute *n*
   /'teknɪkl 'ɪnstɪtjuːt/

there are /ðeə(r) ɑː(r)/
there is /ðeə(r) ɪz/
thing *n* /θɪŋ/
tourists *n pl* /'tʊərɪsts/
travelling *n* /'trævəlɪŋ/
Tunisia *n* /tju'nɪziə/
Uruguay *n* /'jʊərəgwaɪ/
USA *n* /ˌjuː es 'eɪ/
weather *n* /'weðə(r)/
west *n* /west/
Western Sahara *n*
   /'westən sə'hɑːrə/

Unit 3

afternoon *n* /ˌɑːftə'nuːn/
article *n* /'ɑːtɪkl/
at *prep* /æt/
beginning *n* /bɪ'gɪnɪŋ/
box *n* /bɒks/
breakfast *n* /'brekfəst/
business studies *n*
   /'bɪznəs ˌstʌdiz/
cafeteria *n* /ˌkæfə'tɪəriə/
car *n* /kɑː(r)/
chemistry *n* /'kemɪstri/
choose *v* /tʃuːz/
clock *n* /klɒk/
coffee *n* /'kɒfi/
colour *n* /'kʌlə(r)/
compare *v* /kəm'peə(r)/
computer *n* /kəm'pjuːtə(r)/
computer centre *n*
   /kəm'pjuːtə(r) 'sentə(r)/
day *n* /deɪ/
dinner *n* /'dɪnə(r)/
drink *v* /drɪŋk/
drive *v* /draɪv/
each /iːtʃ/
emails *n pl* /'iːmeɪlz/
evening *n* /'iːvnɪŋ/
every day *adv* /'evrideɪ/
false *adj* /fɔːls/
football match *n* /'fʊtbɔːl mætʃ/
French *n* /frentʃ/
Friday *n* /'fraɪdeɪ/
general information *n*
   /'dʒenrəl ˌɪnfə'meɪʃn/
get up *v* /get 'ʌp/
give *v* /gɪv/
go on *v* /gəʊ 'ɒn/
go to *v* /gəʊ tuː/
go together *v* /gəʊ tə'geðə(r)/
group *n* /gruːp/
gym *n* /dʒɪm/
home *n* /həʊm/
homework *n* /'həʊmwɜːk/
how old? /haʊ əʊld/
lab *n* /læb/
language *n* /'læŋgwɪdʒ/
leave *v* /liːv/
lecture *n* /'lektʃə(r)/
library *n* /'laɪbrəri/
look for *v* /'lʊk fɔː(r)/
lunch *n* /lʌntʃ/
make *v* /meɪk/
maths *n* /mæθs/
medicine *n* /'medɪsn/
Monday *n* /'mʌndeɪ/
morning *n* /'mɔːnɪŋ/
multimedia centre *n*
   /ˌmʌlti'miːdiə 'sentə(r)/
note *n* /nəʊt/
nursing *n* /'nɜːsɪŋ/
object *n* /'ɒbdʒɪkt/
order *n* /'ɔːdə(r)/
part *n* /pɑːt/
physics *n* /'fɪzɪks/

preposition *n* /ˌprepə'zɪʃn/
record *v* /rɪ'kɔːd/
remember *v* /rɪ'membə(r)/
research *n* /rɪ'sɜːtʃ/
Saturday *n* /'sætədeɪ/
see *v* /siː/
seminar *n* /'semɪnɑː(r)/
send *v* /send/
simple *adj* /'sɪmpl/
skimming *n* /skɪmɪŋ/
some *adj* /sʌm/
Spanish *n* /'spænɪʃ/
spell check tool *n* /'spel tʃek tuːl/
spelling *n* /'spelɪŋ/
sports programmes *n pl*
   /spɔːts 'prəʊgræmz/
start *v* /stɑːt/
studies *n pl* /'stʌdiz/
Sunday *n* /'sʌndeɪ/
television *n* /'telɪvɪʒn/
Thursday *n* /'θɜːzdeɪ/
time *n* /taɪm/
time expression *n*
   /ˌtaɪm ɪk'spreʃn/
true *adj* /truː/
Tuesday *n* /'tjuːzdeɪ/
TV *n* /ˌtiː 'viː/
under *prep* /'ʌndə(r)/
visit *v* /'vɪzɪt/
vocabulary *n* /və'kæbjələri/
watch *v* /wɒtʃ/
Wednesday *n* /'wenzdeɪ/
week *n* /wiːk/
weekend *n* /ˌwiːk'end/
when? /wen/
work *n* /wɜːk/
writing n /'raɪtɪŋ/

Unit 4

adjective n /'ædʒɪktɪv/
advantage n /əd'vɑːntɪdʒ/
adverb n /'ædvɜːb/
airports n pl /'eəpɔːts/
alone adv /ə'ləʊn/
arrive v /ə'raɪv/

bad adj /bæd/
because conj /bɪ'kɒz/
because of prep /bɪ'kɒz ɒv/
better adj /'betə(r)/
biology n /baɪ'ɒlədʒi/
both /bəʊθ/
bridges n pl /'brɪdʒɪz/
build v /bɪld/
building site n /'bɪldɪŋ saɪt/

can v /kæn/
career n /kə'rɪə(r)/
cheap adj /tʃiːp/
civil engineer n
    /ˌsɪvl endʒɪ'nɪə(r)/
class n /klɑːs/
clean adj /kliːn/
clearer adj /'klɪərə(r)/
companies n pl /'kʌmpəniz/
computer file n /kəm'pjuːtə faɪl/
conclude v /kən'kluːd/

define v /dɪ'faɪn/
design v /dɪ'zaɪn/
difficult adj /'dɪfɪkəlt/
dirty adj /'dɜːti/
disadvantage n /ˌdɪsəd'vɑːntɪdʒ/
drawing n /'drɔːɪŋ/

each other /iːtʃ 'ʌðə(r)/
early adv /'ɜːli/
easily adv /'iːzəli/
easy adj /'iːzi/
electricity n /ɪˌlek'trɪsəti/
ending n /'endɪŋ/
engineering n /ˌendʒɪ'nɪərɪŋ/
English n /'ɪŋglɪʃ/
exercise n /'eksəsaɪz/

family name n /'fæməli ˌneɪm/
famous adj /'feɪməs/
finally adv /'faɪnəli/
first name /'fɜːst ˌneɪm/
firstly adv /'fɜːstli/
free time n /friː taɪm/

get ill /get 'ɪl/
good adj /gʊd/
greater adj /'greɪtə(r)/

health n /helθ/

information n /ˌɪnfə'meɪʃn/

job n /dʒɒb/

law n /lɔː/
lecture theatre n
    /'lektʃə(r) 'θɪətə(r)/
less /les/

more /mɔː(r)/
music n /'mjuːzɪk/

near prep /nɪə(r)/
need v /niːd/
noise n /nɔɪz/
noisy adj /'nɔɪzi/

notebook n /'nəʊtbʊk/
notes n pl /nəʊts/
now adv /naʊ/

open-plan adj /ˌəʊpən 'plæn/
outside adv /ˌaʊt'saɪd/

pair n /peə(r)/
place n /pleɪs/
plan v /plæn/
privately adv /'praɪvətli/
profession n /prə'feʃn/
put v /pʊt/

quiet adj /'kwaɪət/

railways n pl /'reɪlweɪz/
reason n /'riːzn/
record n /'rekɔːd/
researchers n pl /rɪ'sɜːtʃəz/
roads n pl /rəʊdz/
room n /ruːm/

scanning n /'skænɪŋ/
search engine n /ˌsɜːtʃ 'endʒɪn/
secondly adv /'sekəndli/
shop v /ʃɒp/
shopping n /'ʃɒpɪŋ/
show v /ʃəʊ/
silence n /'saɪləns/
small adj /smɔːl/
sometimes adv /'sʌmtaɪmz/
spell v /spel/
sport n /spɔːt/
squash n /skwɒʃ/
study n /'stʌdi/

take v /teɪk/
talk v /tɔːk/
tennis n /'tenɪs/
the same /ðə 'seɪm/
then /ðen/
think v /θɪŋk/
three /θriː/
together adv /tə'geðə(r)/
translation n /træns'leɪʃn/
travel v /'trævl/
types n pl /taɪps/

useful adj /'juːsfl/

want v /wɒnt/
well adv /wel/
why? /waɪ/
work colleagues n pl
    /wɜːk 'kɒliːgz/
work long hours /wɜːk lɒŋ 'aʊəz/
world n /wɜːld/
world language n
    /wɜːld 'læŋgwɪdʒ/

years n pl /jɪəz/

Unit 5

action n /'ækʃn/
address n /ə'dres/
advertisement n /əd'vɜːtɪsmənt/
animals n pl /'ænɪmlz/
application form
    /ˌæplɪ'keɪʃn fɔːm/
assembly point n /ə'sembli pɔɪnt/

bags n pl /bægz/
basketball n /'bɑːskɪtbɔːl/
black n, adj /blæk/
blue n, adj /bluː/
born v /bɔːn/
bring v /brɪŋ/
building n /'bɪldɪŋ/
bus n /bʌs/

calm adj /kɑːm/
circle n /'sɜːkl/
clear adj /klɪə(r)/
clearly adv /'klɪəli/
cross v /krɒs/

danger n /'deɪndʒə(r)/
date of birth n /deɪt ɒv 'bɜːθ/
discuss v /dɪ'skʌs/
documents n pl /'dɒkjuments/

eat v /iːt/
email address n /'iːmeɪl ə'dres/
essay n /'eseɪ/
everyone /'evriwʌn/
exit n /'eksɪt/

fire n /faɪə(r)/
fire alarm n /'faɪər əlɑːm/
follow v /'fɒləʊ/
football n /'fʊtbɔːl/
form n /fɔːm/
formal adj /'fɔːml/

geographical features n pl
    /ˌdʒiːə'græfɪkl 'fiːtʃəz/
go back v /gəʊ 'bæk/
green n /griːn/

hear v /hɪə(r)/
here adv /hɪə(r)/

ink n /ɪŋk/
interested adj /'ɪntrəstɪd/
into prep /'ɪntə/

Japanese adj /ˌdʒæpə'niːz/

landing card n /'lændɪŋ kɑːd/
librarian n /laɪ'breəriən/
lift n /lɪft/
lockers n pl /'lɒkəz/

memory stick n /'meməri stɪk/
mobile phone n /ˌməʊbaɪl 'fəʊn/
nationality n /ˌnæʃə'næləti/
no entry /nəʊ 'entri/
notice n /'nəʊtɪs/

often adv /'ɒfn/

phrases n pl /'freɪzɪz/
place of birth n /pleɪs ɒv 'bɜːθ/
plane n /pleɪn/

rectangle n /'rektæŋgl/
red n /red/
registration form n
    /ˌredʒɪ'streɪʃn fɔːm/

road n /rəʊd/
run v /rʌn/

safety n /'seɪfti/
save v /seɪv/
seconds n pl /'sekəndz/
September n /sep'tembə(r)/
shape n /ʃeɪp/
sign v /saɪn/
signature n /'sɪgnətʃə(r)/
signs n pl /saɪnz/
size n /saɪz/
smoke v /sməʊk/
sports club n /'spɔːts klʌb/
stay v /steɪ/
streets n pl /striːts/
student ID card n
    /'stjuːdnt aɪ 'diː kɑːd/
student identity card n
    /'stjuːdnt aɪ'dentəti kɑːd/
swimming n /'swɪmɪŋ/

table n /'teɪbl/
taxi n /'tæksi/
telephone number n
    /'telɪfəʊn ˌnʌmbə(r)/
tell v /tel/
tick v /tɪk/
today adv /tə'deɪ/
topic n /'tɒpɪk/
town n /taʊn/
train n /treɪn/
triangle n /'traɪæŋgl/
turn off v /tɜːn 'ɒf/

UK n /ˌjuː 'keɪ/
until conj /ən'tɪl/

volleyball n /'vɒlibɔːl/

white n /waɪt/

Unit 6

ago *adv* /ə'gəʊ/
all /ɔːl/
all over the world
    /ɔːl 'əʊvə(r) ðə 'wɜːld/
ancient world *n* /'eɪnʃənt 'wɜːld/
another /ə'nʌðə(r)/
artemisinin *n* /ˌɑːtɪ'miːsɪnɪn/
aspirin *n* /'æsprɪn/
at sea /æt 'siː/
avoid *v* /ə'vɔɪd/

bark *n* /bɑːk/
begin *v* /bɪ'gɪn/
boat *n* /bəʊt/
bones *n pl* /bəʊnz/
British *adj* /'brɪtɪʃ/

call *v* /kɔːl/
carry away *v* /'kæri ə'weɪ/
cause *v* /kɔːz/
CE /ˌsiː 'iː/
century *n* /'sentʃəri/
chapter *n* /'tʃæptə(r)/
chemicals *n pl* /'kemɪklz/
child *n* /tʃaɪld/
common *adj* /'kɒmən/
could *v* /kʊd/

decide *v* /dɪ'saɪd/
develop *v* /dɪ'veləp/
development *n* /dɪ'veləpmənt/
discover *v* /dɪ'skʌvə(r)/
discoveries *n pl* /dɪ'skʌvəriz/
disease *n* /dɪ'ziːz/

early *adj* /'ɜːli/
educate *v* /'edʒukeɪt/
education *n* /ˌedʒu'keɪʃn/
effect *n* /ɪ'fekt/
Egyptian *adj* /i'dʒɪpʃn/
Egyptians *n pl* /i'dʒɪpʃnz/
eighteenth *adj* /ˌeɪ'tiːnθ/
encyclopedia *n* /ɪnˌsaɪklə'piːdiə/
European *adj* /ˌjʊərə'piːən/
Europeans *n pl* /jʊərə'piːənz/
events *n pl* /ɪ'vents/
exams *n pl* /ɪg'zæmz/
experiment *n* /ɪk'sperɪmənt/

finish *v* /'fɪnɪʃ/
first /fɜːst/
food *n* /fuːd/
fruit *n* /fruːt/

Greeks *n pl* /griːks/

healthy *adj* /'helθi/
history *n* /'hɪstri/
hygiene *n* /'haɪdʒiːn/

importance *n* /ɪm'pɔːtns/
improve *v* /ɪm'pruːv/
in place of *prep* /ɪn 'pleɪs ɒv/
increase *v* /ɪn'kriːs/
introduce *v* /ˌɪntrə'djuːs/
irregular *adj* /ɪ'regjələ(r)/

keep *v* /kiːp/

later *adv* /'leɪtə(r)/
leaves *n pl* /liːvz/
lemon juice *n* /'lemən dʒuːs/
life *n* /laɪf/

malaria *n* /mə'leəriə/
medical *adj* /'medɪkl/
meeting *n* /'miːtɪŋ/
Middle East *n* /ˌmɪdl 'iːst/
modern *adj* /'mɒdn/

next *adj* /nekst/

open *v* /'əʊpən/

pain *n* /peɪn/
past *n* /pɑːst/
patient *n* /'peɪʃnt/
phone *n* /fəʊn/
pipes *n pl* /paɪps/
pour *v* /pɔː(r)/
priest *n* /priːst/
problem *n* /'prɒbləm/
pronoun *n* /'prəʊnaʊn/
public baths *n* /ˌpʌblɪk 'bɑːðz/
public health *n* /ˌpʌblɪk 'helθ/

quinine *n* /kwɪ'niːn/

recognize *v* /'rekəgnaɪz/
refer to *v* /rɪ'fɜː(r) tə/
regular *adj* /'regjələ(r)/
related *adj* /rɪ'leɪtɪd/
repeat *v* /rɪ'piːt/
repetition *n* /ˌrepə'tɪʃn/
replace *v* /rɪ'pleɪs/
result *n* /rɪ'zʌlt/
rewrite *v* /ˌriː'raɪt/
rice *n* /raɪs/
Romans *n pl* /'rəʊmənz/

sailor *n* /'seɪlə(r)/
scientist *n* /'saɪəntɪst/
serious *adj* /'sɪəriəs/
skin *n* /skɪn/
sleep *v* /sliːp/
South America *n* /saʊθ ə'merɪkə/
still *adv* /stɪl/
stop *v* /stɒp/
substance *n* /'sʌbstəns/
surgery *n* /'sɜːdʒəri/

teach *v* /tiːtʃ/
treat *v* /triːt/
tree *n* /triː/
trip *n* /trɪp/
tropical *adj* /'trɒpɪkl/
type *n* /taɪp/

vaccine *n* /'væksiːn/
vegetables *n pl* /'vedʒtəblz/
vitamin *n* /'vɪtəmɪn/

water *n* /'wɔːtə(r)/
ways *n pl* /weɪz/
writers *n pl* /'raɪtəz/

yesterday *adv* /'jestədeɪ/

Unit 7

a few /ə 'fjuː/
academic *adj* /ˌækə'demɪk/
achieve *v* /ə'tʃiːv/
age *n* /eɪdʒ/
American *adj* /ə'merɪkən/
Americans *n pl* /ə'merɪkənz/
April *n* /'eɪprəl/
August *n* /'ɔːgəst/

become *v* /bɪ'kʌm/
belong to *v* /bɪ'lɒŋ tə/
board *n* /bɔːd/

carry *v* /'kæri/

date *n* /deɪt/
December *n* /dɪ'sembə(r)/
distance *n* /'dɪstəns/

Earth *n* /ɜːθ/
eighteenth /ˌeɪ'tiːnθ/
eighth /eɪtθ/
electric *adj* /ɪ'lektrɪk/
electronic *adj* /ɪˌlek'trɒnɪk/
England *n* /'ɪŋglənd/

factory worker *n*
    /'fæktəri 'wɜːkə(r)/
February *n* /'februəri/
fifth /fɪfθ/
first /fɜːst/
flight *n* /flaɪt/
fly *v* /flaɪ/
for sure /fə(r) 'ʃʊə(r)/
fourth /fɔːθ/
Frenchman *n* /'frentʃmən/

grand prix *n* /ˌgrã 'priː/
great *adj* /greɪt/
ground *n* /graʊnd/

helicopter *n* /'helɪkɒptə(r)/
hot-air balloon *n*
    /ˌhɒt 'eə bə'luːn/
how long? /haʊ 'lɒŋ/

introduction *n* /ˌɪntrə'dʌkʃn/
invention *n* /ɪn'venʃn/
inventor *n* /ɪn'ventə(r)/

January *n* /'dʒænjuəri/
join *v* /dʒɔɪn/
July *n* /dʒu'laɪ/
June *n* /dʒuːn/

land *v* /lænd/
long-distance *adj* /ˌlɒŋ 'dɪstəns/

March *n* /mɑːtʃ/
May *n* /meɪ/
minutes *n pl* /'mɪnɪts/
months *n pl* /mʌnθs/
moon *n* /muːn/

nineteenth /ˌnaɪn'tiːnθ/
ninth /naɪnθ/
non-stop *adv* /ˌnɒn 'stɒp/
November *n* /nəʊ'vembə(r)/
number *n* /'nʌmbə(r)/

October *n* /ɒk'təʊbə(r)/
ordinal numbers *n pl*
    /ˌɔːdɪnl 'nʌmbəz/

passenger train *n*
    /'pæsɪndʒə(r) treɪn/

pay *v* /peɪ/
person *n* /'pɜːsn/
pilot *n* /'paɪlət/
pioneer *n* /ˌpaɪə'nɪə(r)/
point *n* /pɔɪnt/
presentation *n* /ˌprezn'teɪʃn/
price *n* /praɪs/
professor *n* /prə'fesə(r)/

race *v* /reɪs/
railway *n* /'reɪlweɪ/
return *v* /rɪ'tɜːn/
Russian *n* /'rʌʃn/

sail *v* /seɪl/
second /'sekənd/
September *n* /sep'tembə(r)/
service *n* /'sɜːvɪs/
seventh /'sevnθ/
ships *n pl* /ʃɪps/
single-handed *adv*
    /ˌsɪŋgl 'hændɪd/
sixth /sɪksθ/
space *n* /speɪs/
space programme *n*
    /ˌspeɪs 'prəʊgræm/
spaceship *n* /'speɪsʃɪp/
speed *n* /spiːd/
story *n* /'stɔːri/
successful *adj* /sək'sesfl/

tenth /tenθ/
test *n* /test/
third /θɜːd/
thousands *n* /'θaʊzndz/
transport *n* /'trænspɔːt/
turn to *v* /'tɜːn tə/
tutor *n* /'tjuːtə(r)/
twentieth /'twentiəθ/
twenty-first /ˌtwenti 'fɜːst/

underground train *n*
    /'ʌndəgraʊnd treɪn/

walk *v* /wɔːk/
who? /huː/
win *v* /wɪn/

youngest *adj* /'jʌŋgɪst/

Unit 8

advertise *v* /ˈædvətaɪz/
advertising *n* /ˈædvətaɪzɪŋ/
attach *v* /əˈtætʃ/
benefit from *v* /ˈbenɪfɪt frɒm/
Best wishes /best wɪʃɪz/
book *v* /bʊk/
bread *n* /bred/
business *n* /ˈbɪznəs/
buy *v* /baɪ/
bye /baɪ/
competitions *n pl* /ˌkɒmpəˈtɪʃnz/
conclusion *n* /kənˈkluːʒn/
connect *v* /kəˈnekt/
copy *n* /ˈkɒpi/
Dear /dɪə(r)/
email *v* /ˈiːmeɪl/
entries *n pl* /ˈentriz/
euros *n pl* /ˈjʊərəʊz/
expensive *adj* /ɪkˈspensɪv/
fans *n pl* /fænz/
favourite *adj* /ˈfeɪvərɪt/
friendly *adj* /ˈfrendli/
games *n pl* /geɪmz/
handouts *n pl* /ˈhændaʊts/
hard *adj, adv* /hɑːd/
hats *n pl* /hæts/
heading *n* /ˈhedɪŋ/
hello /həˈləʊ/
how? /haʊ/
ill *adj* /ɪl/
kind *n, adj* /kaɪnd/
late *adj* /leɪt/
logo *n* /ˈləʊgəʊ/
look forward to …
    /lʊk ˈfɔːwəd tə/
marketing *n* /ˈmɑːkɪtɪŋ/
miss *v* /mɪs/
money *n* /ˈmʌni/
mouse *n* /maʊs/
Olympics *n pl* /əˈlɪmpɪks/
only *adv* /ˈəʊnli/
organizations *n pl*
    /ˌɔːgənaɪˈzeɪʃnz/
park *n, v* /pɑːk/
player *n* /ˈpleɪə(r)/
please find attached …
    /pliːz faɪnd əˈtætʃt/
polite *adj* /pəˈlaɪt/
popular *adj* /ˈpɒpjələ(r)/
products *n pl* /ˈprɒdʌkts/
reading list *n* /ˈrediŋ lɪst/
season ticket *n* /ˈsiːzn tɪkɪt/
sell *v* /sel/
Senior Lecturer *n*
    /ˈsiːniə(r) ˈlektʃərə(r)/
shirts *n pl* /ʃɜːts/
sorry /ˈsɒri/
sources *n pl* /ˈsɔːsɪz/
stadium *n* /ˈsteɪdiəm/
summer *n* /ˈsʌmə(r)/
talk *n* /tɔːk/
term *n* /tɜːm/
tickets *n* /ˈtɪkɪts/
top *adj* /tɒp/
twice *adv* /twaɪs/
unkind *adj* /ˌʌnˈkaɪnd/
usually *adv* /ˈjuːʒuəli/
virus *n* /ˈvaɪrəs/
winter *n* /ˈwɪntə(r)/
would like to *v* /wəd ˈlaɪk tə/

Unit 9

agriculture *n* /ˈægrɪkʌltʃə(r)/
Antarctica *n* /ænˈtɑːktɪkə/
apples *n pl* /ˈæplz/
bar chart *n* /ˈbɑː tʃɑːt/
beef *n* /biːf/
bottled water *n* /ˈbɒtld ˈwɔːtə(r)/
change *v* /tʃeɪndʒ/
chart *n* /tʃɑːt/
chicken *n* /ˈtʃɪkɪn/
chocolate *n* /ˈtʃɒklət/
cold *adj* /kəʊld/
complete *adj* /kəmˈpliːt/
connected *adj* /kəˈnektɪd/
contain *v* /kənˈteɪn/
cover *v* /ˈkʌvə(r)/
crops *n pl* /krɒps/
cup *n* /kʌp/
dependent *adj* /dɪˈpendənt/
describe *v* /dɪˈskraɪb/
description *n* /dɪˈskrɪpʃn/
drinking water *n*
    /ˈdrɪŋkɪŋ wɔːtə(r)/
email box *n* /ˈiːmeɪl bɒks/
farming *n* /ˈfɑːmɪŋ/
figures *n pl* /ˈfɪgəz/
finger *n* /ˈfɪŋgə(r)/
Finland *n* /ˈfɪnlənd/
future *n* /ˈfjuːtʃə(r)/
Germany *n* /ˈdʒɜːməni/
global *adj* /ˈgləʊbl/
goods *n pl* /gʊdz/
grow *v* /grəʊ/
high marks *n pl* /haɪ ˈmɑːks/
Hong Kong *n* /hɒŋ ˈkɒŋ/
how much? /haʊ ˈmʌtʃ/
ice *n* /aɪs/
incomplete *adj* /ˌɪnkəmˈpliːt/
independent *adj* /ˌɪndɪˈpendənt/
Indian Ocean *n* /ˌɪndiən ˈəʊʃn/
industry *n* /ˈɪndəstri/
inexpensive *adj* /ˌɪnɪkˈspensɪv/
kilo *n* /ˈkiːləʊ/
litres *n pl* /ˈliːtəz/
main *adj* /meɪn/
minerals *n pl* /ˈmɪnərəlz/
name *v* /neɪm/
nowadays *adv* /ˈnaʊədeɪz/
old *adj* /əʊld/
Oman *n* /əʊˈmɑːn/
pencil *n* /ˈpensl/
plants *n pl* /plɑːnts/
poor *adj* /pɔː(r)/
potatoes *n pl* /pəˈteɪtəʊz/
produce *v* /prəˈdjuːs/
resource *n* /rɪˈsɔːs/
rich *adj* /rɪtʃ/
right *adj* /raɪt/
sea water *n* /ˈsiː wɔːtə(r)/
Southern Ocean *n* /ˈsʌðən ˈəʊʃn/
square kilometres *n pl*
    /skweː ˈkɪləˌmiːtəz/
statistics *n pl* /stəˈtɪstɪks/
sugar *n* /ˈʃʊgə(r)/
surface *n* /ˈsɜːfɪs/
surround *v* /səˈraʊnd/
take care of *v* /teɪk ˈkeə(r) ɒv/

transport *v* /trænˈspɔːt/
unclean *adj* /ˌʌnˈkliːn/
unhealthy *adj* /ʌnˈhelθi/
unimportant *adj* /ˌʌnɪmˈpɔːtnt/
United Arab Emirates *n*
    /juːˌnaɪtɪd ˌærəb ˈemɪrəts/
unpopular *adj* /ʌnˈpɒpjələ(r)/
unsuccessful *adj* /ˌʌnsəkˈsesfl/
use *n* /juːz/
water *v* /ˈwɔːtə(r)/
water sports *n pl*
    /ˈwɔːtə(r) spɔːts/
wet *adj* /wet/
wrong *adj* /rɒŋ/

Unit 10

accurate *adj* /'ækjərət/
achievements *n pl* /ə'tʃiːvmənts/
Americas *n pl* /ə'merɪkəz/
Asia *n* /'eɪʃə/
billion /'bɪljən/
billionaire *n* /ˌbɪljə'neə(r)/
biotech company *n*
    /'baɪəʊtek 'kʌmpəni/
brand *n* /brænd/
businessman *n* /'bɪznəsmæn/
clothing *n* /'kləʊðɪŋ/
co-found *v* /'kəʊ 'faʊnd/
computer games *n pl*
    /kəm'pjuːtə(r) geɪmz/
computer sciences *n pl*
    /kəm'pjuːtə(r) 'saɪənsɪz/
conclude *v* /kən'kluːd/
cool *adj* /kuːl/
creator *n* /kri'eɪtə(r)/
designer *n* /dɪ'zaɪnə(r)/
DVDs *n pl* /ˌdiː viː 'diːz/
efficient *adj* /ɪ'fɪʃnt/
electrical engineering *n*
    /ɪ'lektrɪkl ˌendʒɪ'nɪərɪŋ/
electronics *n pl* /ɪˌlek'trɒnɪks/
email provider *n*
    /'iːmeɪl prə'vaɪdə(r)/
email service *n* /'iːmeɪl 'sə:vɪs/
employ *v* /ɪm'plɔɪ/
exam results *n pl*
    /ɪg'zæm rɪ'zʌlts/
fashion magazine *n*
    /'fæʃn ˌmægə'ziːn/
fashionable *adj* /'fæʃnəbl/
final sentence *n* /'faɪnl 'sentəns/
footballer *n* /'fʊtbɔːlə(r)/
founder *n* /'faʊndə(r)/
garage *n* /'gærɑːʒ/
hand in *v* /hænd 'ɪn/
huge *adj* /hjuːdʒ/
hundreds /'hʌndrədz/
images *n pl* /'ɪmɪdʒɪz/
in total /ɪn 'təʊtl/
interesting *adj* /'ɪntrəstɪŋ/
international *adj* /ˌɪntə'næʃnəl/
leading *adj* /'liːdɪŋ/
little /'lɪtl/
logically *adv* /'lɒdʒɪkli/
love *v* /lʌv/
market *n* /'mɑːkɪt/
middle sentence *n*
    /'mɪdl 'sentəns/
multi-millionaire *n*
    /ˌmʌltimɪljə'neə(r)/
notice *v* /'nəʊtɪs/
ordinary *adj* /'ɔːdnri/
organize *v* /'ɔːgənaɪz/
personal *adj* /'pɜːsənl/
photographs *n pl* /'fəʊtəgrɑːfs/
racing driver *n* /'reɪsɪŋ 'draɪvə(r)/
realize *v* /'rɪəlaɪz/
sales *n pl* /seɪlz/
science *n* /'saɪəns/
search *n* /sɜːtʃ/
search engine *n* /sɜːtʃ 'endʒɪn/
shoes *n pl* /ʃuːz/

shop *n* /ʃɒp/
strange *adj* /streɪndʒ/
success *n* /sək'ses/
supersonic *adj* /ˌsuːpə'sɒnɪk/
technologies *n pl* /tek'nɒlədʒiz/
topic sentence *n* /'tɒpɪk 'sentəns/
translate *v* /træns'leɪt/
T-shirt *n* /'tiː ʃɜːt/
users *n pl* /'juːzəz/
web *n* /web/
well-organized *adj*
    /wel 'ɔːgənaɪzd/
worldwide *adj* /'wɜːldwaɪd/
Zambia *n* /'zæmbiə/

PHONETIC SYMBOLS

Consonants

1	/p/	as in	**pen** /pen/
2	/b/	as in	**big** /bɪg/
3	/t/	as in	**tea** /tiː/
4	/d/	as in	**do** /duː/
5	/k/	as in	**cat** /kæt/
6	/g/	as in	**go** /gəʊ/
7	/f/	as in	**four** /fɔː/
8	/v/	as in	**very** /'veri/
9	/s/	as in	**son** /sʌn/
10	/z/	as in	**zoo** /zuː/
11	/l/	as in	**live** /lɪv/
12	/m/	as in	**my** /maɪ/
13	/n/	as in	**near** /nɪə/
14	/h/	as in	**happy** /'hæpi/
15	/r/	as in	**red** /red/
16	/j/	as in	**yes** /jes/
17	/w/	as in	**want** /wɒnt/
18	/θ/	as in	**thanks** /θæŋks/
19	/ð/	as in	**the** /ðə/
20	/ʃ/	as in	**she** /ʃiː/
21	/ʒ/	as in	**television** /'telɪvɪʒn/
22	/tʃ/	as in	**child** /tʃaɪld/
23	/dʒ/	as in	**German** /'dʒɜːmən/
24	/ŋ/	as in	**English** /'ɪŋglɪʃ/

Vowels

25	/iː/	as in	**see** /siː/
26	/ɪ/	as in	**his** /hɪz/
27	/i/	as in	**twenty** /'twenti/
28	/e/	as in	**ten** /ten/
29	/æ/	as in	**stamp** /stæmp/
30	/ɑː/	as in	**father** /'fɑːðə/
31	/ɒ/	as in	**hot** /hɒt/
32	/ɔː/	as in	**morning** /'mɔːnɪŋ/
33	/ʊ/	as in	**football** /'fʊtbɔːl/
34	/uː/	as in	**you** /juː/
35	/ʌ/	as in	**sun** /sʌn/
36	/ɜː/	as in	**learn** /lɜːn/
37	/ə/	as in	**letter** /'letə/

Diphthongs (two vowels together)

38	/eɪ/	as in	**name** /neɪm/
39	/əʊ/	as in	**no** /nəʊ/
40	/aɪ/	as in	**my** /maɪ/
41	/aʊ/	as in	**how** /haʊ/
42	/ɔɪ/	as in	**boy** /bɔɪ/
43	/ɪə/	as in	**hear** /hɪə/
44	/eə/	as in	**where** /weə/
45	/ʊə/	as in	**tour** /tʊə/

Great Clarendon Street, Oxford, OX2 6DP, United Kingdom

Oxford University Press is a department of the University of Oxford.
It furthers the University's objective of excellence in research, scholarship,
and education by publishing worldwide. Oxford is a registered trade
mark of Oxford University Press in the UK and in certain other countries

© Oxford University Press 2013

The moral rights of the author have been asserted

First published in 2013

2017 2016 2015

10 9 8 7 6 5 4

No unauthorized photocopying

All rights reserved. No part of this publication may be reproduced, stored
in a retrieval system, or transmitted, in any form or by any means, without
the prior permission in writing of Oxford University Press, or as expressly
permitted by law, by licence or under terms agreed with the appropriate
reprographics rights organization. Enquiries concerning reproduction outside
the scope of the above should be sent to the ELT Rights Department, Oxford
University Press, at the address above

You must not circulate this work in any other form and you must impose
this same condition on any acquirer

Links to third party websites are provided by Oxford in good faith and for
information only. Oxford disclaims any responsibility for the materials
contained in any third party website referenced in this work

ISBN: 978 0 19 474168 2

Printed in China

This book is printed on paper from certified and well-managed sources

ACKNOWLEDGEMENTS

Illustrations by: Kathy Baxendale pp.8, 18, 28, 29, 33; Melvyn Evans pp.6, 20, 32;
Chris Pavely pp.10, 11, 13, 15, 45; Gavin Reece p.21

*We would also like to thank the following for permission to reproduce the following
photographs*: Alamy pp.4 (c/Kablonk/Purestock), 5 (books/RubberBall), 7 (students/
GoGo Images Corporation), 7 (family/Stockbroker/MBI), 10 (Spanish landscape/F.
Vrouenraths (Spain), 11 (desert/Prisma Bildagentur AG), 11 (Algiers/Colin
Matthieu/hemis.hr/Hemis), 12 (Canberra/travellinglight), 16 (1/M Itani), 16 (3/
Yuri Arcurs), 18 (trainers/Helen Sessions), 21 (a/Mike Booth), 22 (a/Hufton +
Crow/VIEW Pictures Ltd), 23 (Vladislav Kochelaevskiy), 25 (lecture hall/Sabine
Lubenow), 27 (bridge building/Iain Masterton), 30 (passport control/Gregory
Wrona), 34 (running machine/Cultura Creative), 35 (Ancient Art & Architecture
Collection Ltd), 36 (ancient medicine/The Art Archive), 37 (aspirin/South West
Images Scotland), 40 (b/Dennis Hallinan), 40 (c/RIA Novosti), 41 (c/Pictorial Press
Ltd), 41 (a/H. Armstrong Roberts/ClassicStock), 43 (a/Chris Hellier), 43 (b/World
History Archive), 47 (stadium/Richard Wareham Fotografie (Nieuws), 48 (Jan
Scherders/Tetra Images), 50 (White mouse/Redmond O'Durrell), 51 (screen/Brian
Jackson), 51 (racing car/mark phillips), 52 (Radius Images), 54 (spoon and rice/
lee avison), 54 (single fish/Star Pix), 54 (fish/Chassenet/Photocuisine), 54 (tea/
Viktor Fischer), 54 (Viktor Fischer), 55 (coffee/Juliana Hoffman), 59 (boxes/
Lux Igitur), 63 (shop front/Kumar Sriskandan); Corbis pp.4 (a/Darren Kemper/
Fancy), 19 (David Leahy/cultura), 21 (b/Tim Pannell/Flame), 30 (woman/Ned Frisk
Photography/Spirit), 47 (boy and TV screens/Randy Faris/Crush); 4 (b/PhotoAlto/
Eric Audras), 4 (d/arabianEye), 5 (a/Sam Edwards/OJO Images), 5 (b/Confluence
Pictures/The Image Bank), 9 (woman/Ghislain & Marie David de Lossy/The Image
Bank), 12 (Riyadh/Ayman Aljammaz/Flickr), 13 (Peter Lilja/Stone), 15 (Canadian
plains/Chris Harris/First Light), 16 (2/Westend61), 17 (a/Asia Images Group),
22 (b/Purestock), 22 (c/Cultura/moodboard), 24 (Philip and Karen Smith/Iconica),
25 (library/DAJ), 25 (study bedroom/thenakedsnail/Flickr Select), 27 (helipad/
James Wells/Stone), 34 (vegetable market/Bruno Morand), 36 (modern
laboratory/Assembly/Iconica), 37 (vaccination/Shashank Bengali/MCT via
Getty Images), 39 (Dorling Kindersley), 41 (b/Popperfoto), 47 (businessmen/
Photodisc/Digital Vision), 47 (buying tickets/Alexander Hassenstein/Bongarts),
53 (Symphonie/Photodisc), 54 (bowl of rice/Philip Wilkins/Photolibrary),
54 (loaves/Foodcollection RF), 54 (loaf/Jules Frazier/Photodisc), 58 (PhotoAlto/
Milena Boniek), 60 (Tamara Mellon/Andy Shaw/Bloomberg via Getty Images),
62 (Dibyangshu Sarkar/AFP); iStockphoto pp.27 (woman engineer/Peter Close),
55 (water/subjug); Rex Features pp.9 (man/Markku Ulander), 17 (b/David
Oxberry/Mood Board), 40 (a/CSU Archives/Everett Collection), 45 (Brendan
Beirne), 59 (Jeff Bezos/Sipa Press), 59 (warehouse/Geoffrey Robinson), 60 (Kiran
Mazumdar-Shaw/Gregory Pace/BEI), 63 (Julian Dunkerton/Adrian Sherratt
Photography Ltd), 63 (woman/Sara Jaye Weiss); Royalty-free pp.8 (laptop/David
Cook/www.blueshiftstudios.co.uk), 10 (flag/Graphi-Ogre), 11 (flag/Graphi-Ogre),
15 (flag/Graphi-Ogre), 57 (Corbis/Digital Stock); Science Photo Library p.37 (Mary
Montagu/NYPL); Shutterstock pp.4 (chess pieces/O2creationz), 14 (Yganko)